Language and Language Disorders in Childhood

EDITED BY

L.A. HERSOV
The Maudsley Hospital, London

and

M. BERGER
University of London Institute of Education

Associate Editor

A. R. NICOL
Nuffield Psychology & Psychiatry Unit, Newcastle-upon-Tyne

PERGAMON PRESS
OXFORD · NEW YORK · TORONTO ·SYDNEY · PARIS · FRANKFURT

U.K.	Pergamon Press Ltd., Headington Hill Hall, Oxford OX3 0BW, England
U.S.A.	Pergamon Press Inc., Maxwell House, Fairview Park, Elmsford, New York 10523, U.S.A.
CANADA	Pergamon of Canada, Suite 104, Consumers Road, Willowdale, Ontario M2J 1P9
AUSTRALIA	Pergamon Press (Aust.) Pty Ltd., P.O. Box 544, Potts Point, N.S.W. 2011, Australia
FRANCE	Pergamon Press SARL, 24 rue des Ecoles, 75240 Paris, Cedex 05, France
FEDERAL REPUBLIC OF GERMANY	Pergamon Press GmbH, 6242 Kronberg/Taunus, Pferdstrasse 1, Federal Republic of Germany

First edition 1980

British Library Cataloguing in Publication Data

Language and language disorders in childhood.
('Journal of child psychology and psychiatry' supplements; no. 2).
1.   Children – Language
I.   Hersov, Lionel Abraham
II.   Berger, M. III. Nicol, Archibald Russell
IV.   Series
401'.9   LB1139.L3   79–40805

ISBN 0 08 025206 0 (Hardcover)
ISBN 0 08 025205 2 (Flexicover)

Book Supplement to the
Journal of Child Psychology and Psychiatry, No. 2.

*Printed and bound in Great Britain by
William Clowes (Beccles) Limited, Beccles and London*

Contents

Introduction to the Series

L. A. HERSOV AND M. BERGER

The Association for Child Psychology and Psychiatry, a learned society, was founded in 1956 to further the scientific study of all matters concerning the mental health and development of children through the medium of meetings and the establishment of a journal. The *Journal of Child Psychology and Psychiatry and Allied Disciplines* was first published in 1960 in conjunction with Pergamon Press and this fruitful collaboration has continued over the years.

The journal is primarily concerned with clinical experimental and developmental studies in child psychology and psychiatry, but its Editors have always recognised the important contributions of other disciplines and other points of view. They have aimed to bring together knowledge from related fields of animal behaviour, anthropology, education, family studies, sociology, physiology and paediatrics in order to promote an eventual integration.

We can claim some success in this endeavour, but have been aware of the need to supplement the material in the Journal with a publication which would bring together, under one cover, research studies on one particular topic or the contributions to a symposium or conference on a particular theme.

In recent years the officers of the Association have considered ways and means of bringing such a publication to the membership and to a wider readership of professional workers in the various disciplines concerned with child health, development, education and care. The Association and Pergamon Press began publishing supplements to the Journal in 1978. These will appear from time to time under the general Editorship of the Editors of the Journal with the help of an Associate Editor when needed.

The Editors invite contributions of high quality from clinicians and research workers who wish to publish their studies in a single volume, as well as the proceedings of conferences and symposia on themes related to child psychology, psychiatry and allied disciplines. All submissions will be assessed through the normal refereeing process.

Lionel Hersov
Michael Berger

Joint Editors
*Journal of Child Psychology and
Psychiatry and Allied Disciplines*

Introduction to the Volume

A. R. NICOL

Language disorders are a source of distress and social handicap. There are many areas in this broad field where clinical problems can be illuminated by an understanding of both recent research findings and current academic debates. The potential benefits are rich as there has been an intense concentration of research interest on various facets of language over the last 20 years. It is the object of this monograph to bring some of these findings and debates to a clinical audience. The papers here were first presented at a conference convened by the child Psychiatry Specialist Section of the Royal College of Psychiatrists in March 1978.

In the field of child development, understanding of normal and abnormal functioning advances by mutual cross-fertilisation. In the first review, Cromer surveys some conceptual problems and then shows how one may go about studying the way in which both very young and language-impaired children learn the rules of language. The importance of these techniques in studying clinical groups is not hard to see although the applications are still largely for future use. Of particular interest are the findings of individual strategies that children use in trying to get to grips with complex language structures. Perhaps this sort of knowledge will help in developing remedial programmes.

An understanding of social influences on language development is of central relevance, both when trying to disentangle aetiological influences and when planning management of children with a wide range of disadvantages and difficulties. Robinson brings a fresh perspective to the long standing debate over socioeconomic status, language and education in his discussion of the competitive nature of the educational system. His analysis of the implications of this simple but often ignored fact has direct importance to clinicians who are frequently called on to help the "misfits" of the system. The work of Tizard and her colleagues on the quality of language provided in the home and nursery school settings forces us to review the commonly held belief that nursery education is always helpful to the language-retarded child.

The later chapters deal with clinical issues. The first essential is to have a convenient means of describing the clinical entities we see. Martin tackles this problem by providing a profile of various levels of disability. He applies his method to a clinical sample and is able by this means to delineate different syndromes in the case material. Fundudis and his colleagues present data from their follow up of the speech retarded children identified in the Newcastle Child Development Study. This provides an important longitudinal view of the outcome in various diagnostic groups of disorders as well as information on their prevalence.

The final two chapters concern treatment of what is widely seen as the most profound of the language disorders, Infantile Autism. Howlin's paper reports a home-based language programme which used a variety of behavioural treatment strategies with autistic children and their mothers. Finally, Rutter uses data from the same study as a starting point for a wider ranging discussion of the acquisition of autistic and normal speech. He focuses attention on language development as an aspect of social interaction and communication, thus complementing the individual structural development discussed by Cromer.

These three rich and closely argued reviews and four research reports bear witness to the advances that have been made in this field and augur well for the future.

A. R. Nicol
Nuffield Psychology and Psychiatry unit,
Newcastle-upon-Tyne.

CHAPTER 1

Normal Language Development: Recent Progress

RICHARD F. CROMER

Medical Research Council Developmental Psychology Unit, London.

When I set about to review the topic, "Normal Language Development: Recent Progress", two questions immediately arose: first, what is meant by "language", and second, what is meant by "progress"? In my brief, I was asked to evaluate how some of the theories of language development over the last twenty years are faring in the light of research evidence. Over these years, however, the conception of "language" has changed. Some changes in what is studied as "language" represent progress in the sense that new and important areas are being explored. But some of the changes also represent a degree of frustration at the lack of real progress on the manner of acquisition of language as originally defined. It may even be that students and newcomers to this field are unaware of these frustrations — i.e., unaware that the problems that the structure of language raised for various theories of acquisition remain yet unsolved. These are the issues I want to address. In order to do this, it is necessary to go back to the late 1950s to see exactly what were the original problems to which attention was directed and to gauge more recent approaches in dealing with them.

When the problem of language acquisition was posed in the 1950s, it was in the form of the acquisition of the structures of the language — i.e., the syntax. In 1957, B. F. Skinner published *Verbal Behavior*, a book which was the culmination of the development of the theory that had dominated psychological research for the prior half century. In

1

that book Skinner attempted to account for the child's learning of the grammar of his language. This seems an eminently sensible thing for a learning theorist to study since it is obvious that languages differ, and children acquire the language to which they are exposed. Skinner, and those who followed his line of thought in modified versions, had both a conceptualisation of the structure of language and a postulated set of mechanisms for the acquisition of that structure. It will be clearer if these two aspects — a theory of structure and a set of mechanisms for acquiring that structure — are treated separately.

The theoretical apparatus, which for sake of simplicity we can call simply the behaviourist view, treated language structure as a set of sequential units held together by associations. Language was seen entirely in terms of its spoken or written units — i.e., in terms of what has come to be called its surface form. Let us see what types of theories this conception of language structure leads to and why they have been criticised by linguists and psycholinguists. Many people "know" that the behaviourist or associationistic theory of language structure is inadequate, but they have no clear idea why this is so; they have merely accepted that it is inadequate because introductory texts in psycholinguistics have said so. As I will point out near the end of this paper, several of the more recent theories of language acquisition which seem to explain much more about language in that they take account of properties other than syntactic structure, end up with conceptual errors similar to those that make associationistic theories inadequate.

Skinner originally held that every word and every acceptable combination of words would have to have been learned through the processes of discrimination learning. All words and multi-word utterances would have been learned separately and made to occur in appropriate situations through reinforcement. A child, for example, would imitate parts of utterances he hears. Notions such as the frequency of various types of utterances would be important in determining his learning. He would be reinforced in various ways by his parents and other adults in learning the language. The use of these responses by the child, i.e., practice, would be another important variable. We will examine the evidence for these processes of imitation, frequency, practice and reinforcement further on. For now, let us examine the structure of language to which this theory leads.

First, if every combination of words had to be learned separately, then language would be made up of a finite number of forms. Those structures used by people would have to have been heard in the course of acquisition and according to the theory must have been involved in some reward structure as well. George Miller (1964) once made a calculation concerning English. He estimated that there are at least 1,000 sentences 20 words long, and if a child were to learn only these it would take him something of the order of 100,000,000,000 centuries, that is 1,000 times the estimated age of the earth, just to listen to them. In other words, the important thing about language is that the grammatical structures that can be created within a language are infinite. Only a tiny portion of these will have ever occurred as actual stimuli or responses. What one needs then is a generative grammar, i.e., a set of rules that by their application will generate all the acceptable combinations in that language and will not generate ungrammatical combinations.

Other theorists attempted to circumvent this problem by increasing the power of an associative theory. Jenkins and Palermo (1964), for example, attempted an explanation based on mediated stimulus-response connections, and Braine (1963) used the notion of context generalisation. These theories had in common that the child learned to place words in grammatical categories due to their positions in sentence paradigms. Thus, the child eventually associated not the position of *words*, but the position of *grammatical categories*. If the child has the rule that a noun can be followed by a verb and then an adverb, he can produce the sentence "John runs fast". When, by sentence position, he learns that "Mary" can fit in the noun category, he can then produce "Mary runs fast", and so on. In other words he need not have heard all of the combinations of words, but merely the combinations of grammatical categories which are allowable.

The problem with such a theory is that although it appears to simplify the learning to a manageable degree, in reality it does not. It still treats language as a finite state system. Instead of discrete words constituting the states, grammatical classes do so. These grammatical classes are then connected by associations. In this theory, then, the child needs only to have learned all of the associations among grammatical classes that are allowable in his native language. Miller and Chomsky (1963) pointed out why this theory too is inadequate. They gave as their example the sentence "The people who called and wanted to rent your house when you go away next year are from California". In this 19 word sentence, there is a dependency between the 2nd word and the 19th word — between "people" and "are". You can sense this immediately if the sentence incorrectly were "The people who called and wanted to rent your house when you go away next year *is* from California". Now in order to detect this dependency, the listener must have learned a unique set of associations covering 15 grammatical categories: that an article can be followed by a noun, then a relative, then a verb, then a conjunction, then another verb, and so on. Miller and Chomsky then argued that in any given context, on average there might be about four alternative categories that might follow. Based on this conservative estimate the detection of the dependency between "people" and "are" means that one would have had to have learned 4^{15}, that is, 10^9 different transitions, in a childhood lasting only 10^8 seconds. Learning language structure solely by associative linkages among the words is clearly impossible.

Even if one adds notions such as context generalisation, or notions of "autoclitic responses" (a Skinnerian notion in which one bit of verbal behaviour can depend on other verbal behaviour), such theories cannot deal with the structures of natural language. The basic reason for this is the impossibility of accounting for language structures in terms of surface feature representations. There are two reasons why this is so. First, one word order can convey two or more different grammatical relations. To make this clear, psycholinguists have often cited ambiguous sentences, for in such cases not only the word orders, but the very words are the same. Thus, one used to be treated to examples such as "They are charming snakes", "They are flying planes", or "They are cooking apples" in which "they" referred within the sentence to the final noun, or else to people outside the sentence involved with activities affecting the noun; or more recently to sentences such as "Anne loves horses more than Mark", the interpretation of which I leave to the reader. But such ambiguous structures are not rare accidents. Rather, they illustrate in the clearest way that different grammatical functions can be indicated with the same ordering of surface elements. There are hundreds of other examples of this phenomenon which do not involve ambiguity. The much used example "John is eager to please" and "John is easy to please" illustrates the same idea. In the first, John is the real subject or actor; in the second, the speaker of English realises that someone else pleases John, that John is acted upon. In "John appeared to Bill to like himself", himself is known to refer to "John". But in "John appealed to Bill to like himself", himself now refers to "Bill", in spite of identical surface category orders. Any theory concerned merely with surface word orders is unable to deal with the interpretations of many normal sentences.

Second, the same grammatical relations can be conveyed by varying word or category orders. Take the following set of sentences:

John gave the gift to Mary
John gave Mary the gift
Mary was given the gift by John
The gift was given by John to Mary
The gift was given to Mary by John

In spite of the differing orders, "John" functions as the subject, "gift" as the direct object, and "Mary" as the indirect object.

In summary, linear order is not enough to account for grammatical relations. This can be shown both in the fact that one order can convey several grammatical meanings, and the same grammatical meanings can be conveyed by differing orders. In other words the surface features are not sufficient to define the basic grammatical relations of sentences. What modern linguists do is to hypothesise abstract representations of sentences which define the basic grammatical relations. This, basically, marked the most crucial change that transformational grammar introduced. Although there are many conflicting theories as to the correct representation, most modern linguistic theories hypothesise some sort of abstract representations displaying significant properties of the sentence. In Chomsky's original formulation, these abstract representations were of two types — surface structures and deep structures. For some theorists, the deep structures were purely grammatical; for others, they were semantic; and for others they were a mixture. These abstract representations are transformed into surface strings when a person produces language. When a person comprehends an utterance, he is said to be converting the surface string into underlying surface and deep structures in order to recover basic meanings. Note that such a theory does not deny that properties of surface strings affect meaning. It only entails that part of the basic process is the recovery of an abstract representation. This may be accomplished by various means. More recent theories of trace grammar (Chomsky, 1975) and "realistic transformational grammar" which is compatible with augmented transition networks (Bresnan, 1978) place more emphasis on surface structures which are themselves abstract representations of surface strings.

Originally, many linguists represented the conversion process between underlying and surface structures by postulating a series of transformations. That such representations may be necessary for linguists to describe adult language is one thing. That children (or even adults) use these representations to produce the utterances they make is quite a different claim. A number of experiments in the early 1960s resulted in conflicting evidence. At first there was some support for claiming that transformations had some psychological reality (McMahon, 1963; Mehler, 1963; Miller & McKean, 1964; Savin & Perchonock, 1963). Later experiments, however, cast some doubt on this assumption (Fodor & Garrett, 1967; Slobin, 1966, 1968; and see discussion in Fodor & Garrett, 1966). It is now generally accepted that production processes are more complex than formerly believed, and many factors other than transformational structure play a vital part. Indeed, it is even questioned whether transformational complexity plays any part in production processes; in some modern theories, as mentioned above (Bresnan, 1978; Chomsky, 1975), transformations play a reduced role. Nevertheless, linguistic evidence from adults supports the notion that adults do have an abstract representation of structure. The problems of the representation of this knowledge are discussed in a thorough review by Watt (1970). The major problem is that people do not seem to go through the steps required by some transformational theories in order to arrive at the surface structure that represents their utterances. It there are a greater number of steps in the derivation of one structure than another, then it should be reflected in greater processing time for the structure with the greater number of steps. This is often not the case, however. The point is that we simply do not know how people comprehend or produce sentences. But we do know that people have some sort of abstract representation of structures and that linguistic forms are interrelated in ways not revealed by surface features. I have argued so far only that this notion is theoretically necessary. But careful studies of child language also show that children organise their knowledge of linguistic structure, as evidenced in their productions, in terms of complex interrelations. It will be useful, therefore, to look at some examples from real children to see more precisely what is meant.

Bellugi-Klima (1969) noted an interesting phenomenon in children acquiring auxiliaries. If the child's utterances are studied closely at one point in time, say at the age of two years, the various common auxiliaries such as "will" and "can" and "do" are lacking. However, looked at only a few months later, say at age two years and three months, the child's language production contains all the common auxiliaries. Where earlier the child had made declarative utterances without auxiliaries, as in "He go", "She come", now these are produced with the auxiliary: "He can go", "She will come". Furthermore, the auxiliaries appear in a variety of structures. Not only are they found in declaratives, but in questions too, and, at least in yes/no questions, they are inverted with the subject noun phrase. The child now produces "Can he do it?" in which the auxiliary has been transferred from its position in "He can do it". Furthermore, in this inversion, the child provides the "do" form if no auxiliary occurs in the declarative. "He wants it" is uttered as "Does he want it?" in the question form. Note that it is not being said that the child first produced the declarative form. Rather, he acts as if he had an abstract underlying declarative form from which he extracts the appropriate auxiliary which he then transposes with the noun phrase. He also notices the lack of an auxiliary and produces a form of "do" in that case. It is also at this same stage of language acquisition that auxiliaries are found for the first time in negatives. Real combinations of "not" and an auxiliary are used to form "won't", "couldn't", "isn't", etc. Earlier use of some of what appeared to be auxiliaries such as "can't" were in fact merely vocabulary items. This can be seen in utterances such as "Why not cracker can't talk?". At the present stage, when true auxiliaries came to be used and were found in a variety of structures, there was no longer any use of "no" or "not" when a negative auxiliary like "can't" was used, at least in the dialect Bellugi was studying. The common auxiliaries, then, appeared in the same stage of the child's language acquisition, and did so in a variety of linguistic structures. As Bellugi put it, "In terms of learning theory based on frequency of occurrence, transition probabilities, reinforcement contingencies, etc., there is absolutely no reason to expect the appearance of grammatically based processes across the board and at one period in the child's speech."

There are other ways that one can notice the interrelationships of auxiliary forms in child speech. Some auxiliaries, like "will" are almost invariably contracted in declarative sentences by adults. Bellugi-Klima (1969) noted a number of examples from the mother of Eve, one of the children studied by Roger Brown and his associates. Notice the different forms the contraction " 'll" takes:

I'll have to invest in a new dishpan
She'll repeat that
Oh we'll have to look
You'll ruin it
That'll be enough

The child, at this stage, does not produce the contraction. Instead, she uses the full form of the auxiliary, making her speech sound somewhat more precise than that of adults:

I will stand on my knees
We will buy Becky a new one
He will have some
It will work on here, see?

The child produces this non-contracted form of "will" in her declarative sentences even though in the speech she hears the adults almost invariably used the contracted form. How does the child do this? It should be noted that the mother does produce the full form, "will", but this occurs in questions: "Will it be fun?", "Will you finish it?". Bellugi argues that the child apparently has analysed the mother's declarative forms such as "I'll" and "he'll" as containing two morphemes: a pronoun and a preverbal form, "will". The adult uses the full form of "will' only in questions. In the child's speech, however, the full form is used in both questions and statements — suggesting that they are organised together by the child.

These few examples are intended to give some idea of what is meant by the observation that children organise the structure of their language in interrelated ways. In any event, this can be shown as necessary for a description of adult utterances, and children must eventually acquire that competence. Now we have some notion of the complexity of that system — a system quite unlike that envisaged by the older behaviourist theories of the associations among successive elements. This constituted a major change in the conception of *what* must be acquired; but equally important, we must turn to the problem of *how* such a system is acquired.

It has been argued for some time now that the general principles used to account for human learning are by themselves inadequate to explain the language acquisition process. The examples given earlier show that the child progresses through a number of stages. His errors are evidence of the rule system he has constructed at any given point. What he produces, then, are not imitations of adult structure, but the utterances which result from his own rule system. Note that this is not to claim that imitation has no role to play in language acquisition or use. Nor, despite polemics to the contrary, has anyone made that claim. Children do imitate, and those imitations no doubt serve important functions. But imitation in the sense originally used by the behaviourists to explain language acquisition is inadequate to explain that process. It is not even adequate to explain the acquisition of the child's first words (see Ricks, 1972). Similarly, notions such as frequency and practice are not central to language acquisition. Brown (1973) found that the frequency with which mothers used certain forms correlated only .26 with the order of acquisition of those forms by their children. It has also been observed (Frith, personal communication) that with children brought up bilingually, large daily differences in exposure to the two languages they are acquiring does not necessarily lead to comparable differences in their competence in those languages. Finally, the principle of reinforcement has often been invoked to explain language acquisition. Reinforcement can indeed be shown to have an effect on verbal behaviour, but again it seems not to be through reinforcement that language structures are acquired. Brown and Hanlon (1970) reported that mothers mainly reinforced for truth value, and very rarely for syntax.

How, then, do children acquire the structure of language? Other notions that have been put forward include the hypothesis that much of language acquisition relies on innate processes (McNeill, 1970a, 1970b). This has been treated with some disdain by psychologists who nevertheless are content to accept innate perceptual mechanisms and their effect on vision. If by innate is meant the various neurological underpinnings necessary for language, not only is this notion plausible, but our attention may be directed to uncovering basic problems in language acquisition in developmentally aphasic children and in autistic children. Even if innate is taken to indicate the more structural/functional aspects of the linguistic code itself, the issue is far more complex than we are led to believe by those who would dismiss it outright since it goes against their philosophical view of the human mind (see Chomsky, 1966, 1968, for a discussion).

At the other extreme, environmental proposals have been put forward to help account for language acquisition. These have included a notion of "expansions" in which the mother or other adult expands the child's short utterances into more complex forms (Brown & Bellugi, 1964; Cazden, 1965). By this means the child is able to observe a model utterance which supplies the morphemes the child has eliminated. Brown (1968) has also speculated on various types of "promptings" given by the adult. For example, if the mother's question "What do you want?" elicits no response from the child, she may then say, "You want what?". Through such means the child could come to learn the equivalence between question forms. Ideas such as these are interesting. There has been to date, however, no conclusive demonstration of the significance of such mechanisms for language acquisition.

The change in outlook from viewing the child as a passive organism absorbing language to one in which the child plays the active role, has in turn led to a shift in the conceptualisation of the mechanisms by which the child acquires his linguistic structures. There has been a growing interest in what are referred to as "language acquisition strategies". This conceptualisation stems from the influential work on concept formation by adults by Bruner, Goodnow and Austin (1956). Essentially the child is seen as acquiring language structures through a kind of problem-solving or concept formation process. Much of this more recent research concentrates on the acquisition of particular structures. The acquisition of specific structures can be closely observed, experimented upon, and perhaps explained (see Cromer, 1976b for a full discussion and review of strategies for language acquisition). Children may use many different strategies for acquiring the structures of their native language. One of these has been called the probable event strategy. Strohner and Nelson (1974) found that children of two and three years of age often performed incorrectly with what they called improbable active sentences. For example, asked to show "The fence jumps over the horse", these children would often manipulate the toys so as to show the horse jumping over the fence. By the age of five years, however, children no longer relied on this strategy. Instead, they used the order of words correctly to interpret the sentence — and this in spite of knowing much more about real event probabilities in the world at the older age. Hazel Dewart (1975) even showed that probability could be affected by the use of a short linguistic frame. Children between 3½ and 4½ years of age who in a pretest condition were shown not to understand passive sentence constructions, were influenced by the appropriateness and inappropriateness of surrounding contexts. For example, whereas for the appropriate context, the child would hear "Poor duck; the duck is bitten by the monkey", for the inappropriate context he would hear "Poor monkey; the duck is bitten by the monkey". In the no context or inappropriate context conditions children gave 2 per cent and 10 per cent correct responses. By contrast these children scored 37 per cent correct responses on passive sentences when they were influenced by an appropriate context.

Some children use what Donaldson and McGarrigle (1974) called "local rules" for interpretation in comprehension tasks. In one of their experiments, children were presented with five cars on one shelf and four cars on another. They would correctly answer that the first shelf had "more". In some conditions, a garage structure was placed over the cars. The shelf with five cars had four garages. When the children were asked which shelf had more cars, a significant number now replied that the shelf with four cars had "more", because now there were "enough to go in there". In other words, "more" meant longer when no garages were present, but "more" meant the garage structure which was full but shorter when the garage structure was in place. This is an example of a "local rule" which interacts with lexical and syntactic rules. A local rule, then, is an extralinguistic strategy to interpret words or sentences.

Some local rules may be very specific. Eve Clark (1973b) studied the interpretations of "in", "on" and "under" by children between 1½ and 5 years of age. The children had to place animals in or on a box which was on its side, in or under an open-backed lorry, and on or under a table. Within these contrasts some young children performed 100 per cent correctly on "in", 50 per cent correctly on "on" and never correctly interpreted "under". Rather than interpreting the results as showing that children had acquired the meaning of "in", were beginning to understand "on", and had no idea of the meaning of "under", she realised that the same results would be obtained if the child operated as if he had two ordered rules. The first is, if the reference point (where the object is to be placed) is a container, put the object "in" it. Second, if the reference point has a horizontal surface, put the object "on" it. By using these two rules, children will perform correctly on all contrasts containing "in". Furthermore, whenever "in" and "on" are contrasted, they will get "on" wrong (since they will place all objects "in" the container regardless of the word used); but when "on" is contrasted with "under", they will get "on" correct (since they will place all objects "on" a horizontal surface regardless of the word used). This will lead to 50 per cent correct replies for "on" in her experiment, while "under" will never be correctly performed. Clark then went on to show that young children used these strategies in other situations.

Huttenlocher and her associates have demonstrated that children will often make the easiest motor response in carrying out a task of linguistic interpretation. For example, given a task in which the child must show his interpretation, the instruction to make the display so that "the red block is on top of the green block" was found to be easier if the child was holding the red block than if he was holding the green block (Huttenlocher & Strauss, 1968). In another experiment in which active and passive sentences were used (Huttenlocher, Eisenberg, & Strauss, 1968), children held one of the two objects in the sentence in their hand. Active sentences were more easily performed if the object the child held was the grammatical subject. With passive sentences, however, it was easier to place the object held in the hand if it was the grammatical object (i.e., the logical subject or real actor) of the sentence. In other words, children prefer to make the easiest motor response and thus perform an action with the object already in their hand. These experiments were conducted with children nine and ten years of age. Dewart (1975) obtained a similar result with four-, five- and six-year-olds on passive sentences. Some children who did not yet know the passive construction used a strategy of interpreting all passive sentences by treating the toy held in their hand as the actor for all sentences.

Children also make use of a number of perceptual processing strategies for interpreting sentences. Bever (1970) has noted that some self-embedded sentences are more difficult than others. On a purely structural basis, there is no reason to expect such differences. Bever gives as an example the sentence, "The dog the cat was scratching was yelping". He points out that in this sentence, the first noun phrase ("the dog") serves a double function. It is the subject of the main sentence ("The dog was yelping") but at the same time, it is the object of the internal sentence ("The cat was scratching the dog"). And this accounts for the difficulty. It is hard to perceive a unit as having two positions on the same classificatory dimension.

The same type of problem has been studied by Amy Sheldon (1974) using sentences with relative clauses and co-referential nominals. Take for example the sentence "The dog that jumps over the pig bumps into the lion". Notice that the dog functions as a subject in both clauses: the dog jumps over the pig, and the dog bumps into the lion. Sheldon refers to this as "parallel function". Such sentences can be contrasted with those with non-parallel function. For example, in "the lion that the horse bumps into jumps over the giraffe", it is the horse that bumps into the lion; lion is the object of the first clause. But it is the lion that jumps over the giraffe; the lion now changes roles and becomes the subject in the second clause. Sheldon demonstrated that children between 3½ and 5½ years of age performed significantly better on sentences with parallel function than on sentences with non-parallel function when asked to carry out the actions with toy animals.

There are several other strategies that children have been found to use at different ages. For example, Bever, Mehler and Valian (1968) discovered that four-year-old children make use of word order clues such that the first noun in a sentence is treated as the actor. They therefore go through a stage of misinterpreting passive sentences. Dewart (1975) has found this to be the most common strategy for interpreting a number of other linguistic constructions as well. However, Dewart's experiments also showed that while this was the most common strategy, some children used other strategies for the same sentence structures. She included sentences with two objects (e.g., "Send the cat to the dog") and instrumental sentences (e.g., "Hit the dog with the cat"). Children had to interpret these sentences when they were presented with various distorted word orders, as in "Send to the dog the cat", "The cat to the dog send", "The cat send to the dog", etc. Thus, although treating the first noun as the one to be moved was found to be the most commonly used strategy, some children consistently moved the noun nearest the verb; others consistently moved the noun not marked by the word "to"; and some even used the strategy that the second noun was the one to be moved. In other words, children exhibit individual differences in the strategies they use for comprehending sentences in such experiments.

In spontaneous production, children also exhibit individual differences. Katherine Nelson (1973) found that some children's first words were predominantly referential. That is, they were mainly the names of objects. By contrast, other children's first words were what Nelson called expressive. These children first used words of a personal or social type for expressing feelings and needs. Nelson also found individual differences in the overall manner of language use. Some children used a production strategy in which they tried out their primitive conceptions of sentences against acceptance by the people around them in their environment. Other children, by contrast, used a comprehension strategy. They would not try out their sentences. Instead, they began to use structures "all-of-a-sudden".

These, then, are some of the strategies that have been studied. It can be noted that the notion of strategy use has led to a closer investigation of specific linguistic structures. It has also led to a greater appreciation of individual differences in comprehension and production. What has it told us about the *acquisition* of linguistic structure, however? If one stops to examine why strategies are used by children to interpret sentences, a peculiar fact becomes apparent. Children who know the linguistic structure being examined perform correctly. For those who do not yet comprehend that structure, however, a strategy constitutes a method for answering the psycholinguist's strange probings; strategies are used when the child does not know what else to do. In other words, the conceptualisation of strategies children use in performing linguistic tasks represents an advance in that the child is now seen as an active organism interacting with the world. It has led to a number of important discoveries, not the least of which is the significance of individual differences in language use. But evaluated in terms of explaining the acquisition of language structure itself, progress may be illusory.

Another approach to language acquisition has been to try to understand some of the necessary cognitive prerequisites for language. These approaches may be of most use for those dealing with child language disorders. For example, Menyuk (1964, 1969) has hypothesised that a short term memory deficit may be responsible for the deviant language structures she observed in a group of children aged three to six years whose language had originally been labelled as infantile. In a repetition task, normal-speaking children were affected by syntactic structure, not by sentence length. The imitations by the language-deviant group, by contrast, were mainly constrained by sentence length. Short term memory even for utterances as short as three to five morphemes in length was found to be impaired. If children can keep in memory no more than two or three morphemes, they will be limited in the kind of linguistic analysis they can perform on the linguistic data to which they are exposed. Menyuk claims that this would result not merely in impoverished and limited language, but in language based on hypotheses and rules differing from those used by children with normal short term memory. Graham (1968, 1974; Graham & Gulliford, 1968) has also put forward a hypothesis concerning the effect of short term memory impairment on language in mentally subnormal children.

Various theories have been proposed to account for the severe problems with language acquisition by developmentally aphasic children. Efron (1963) had noticed that some adult aphasics were unable to judge which of two sounds occurred first unless they were separated by a gap significantly in excess of that usually found between sound segments in speech. Lowe and Campbell (1965) extended this observation to a group of children labelled "aphasoid". They found that whereas their normal-speaking control group required a gap of 30 msec between sounds in order to state which came first, the aphasoid children required on average 350 msec to make this same temporal order judgement. In a series of well-designed experiments, Tallal and Piercy (1973a, b; 1974; 1975) have found that developmentally aphasic children suffer from a sequencing deficit. This they attribute, however, to a more basic deficit in the rate of auditory processing. Based on an analysis of written stories by developmentally aphasic children with virtually no comprehension or production or oral language, I have hypothesised that the underlying deficit may not be a sequencing deficit, but an inability to deal with hierarchically structured material (Cromer, 1979).

An improved understanding of the reasons for language impairment in various clinical groups represents progress which could lead to innovations in dealing with language disorders. Underlying deficits may be responsible for the lack of language acquisition in one or another group. Ways may be suggested for making language available to these groups which bypass their specific disabilities. But again, if we ask the question, what have we learned about the normal acquisition of linguistic structure in unimpaired individuals (or even in language-disordered groups if means are found to bypass their impairments), then we are still faced with the conclusion that we have not progressed very far.

A good deal of work has been done on other cognitive mechanisms that may be responsible for the acquisition of various aspects of linguistic structure. Some of these have been within the Piagetian framework. It has been argued that the cognitive abilities that arise with sensorimotor intelligence are necessary for language acquisition to begin (Sinclair, 1971). The achievement of operational thinking has been claimed to have an important effect on language structures used by children. Sinclair (1969) has reported differences in structures used for describing experimental materials differing in more than one dimension by non-conserving and conserving children on Piaget's famous task. Ferreiro and Sinclair (1971) reported that non-operational children were unable to reverse linguistically the order of two events in time.

The case for the cognitive prerequisites for language acquisition has been made elsewhere (Beilin, 1975; Cromer, 1974; 1976a; Macnamara, 1972). Theories of this type are faced with a dilemma, however. It is possible to claim that certain cognitive mechanisms are *necessary* for language acquisition, but this is different from the claim that they are *sufficient* to explain that acquisition. The applications of cognitive theories to language acquisition have often ignored the problems posed at the beginning of this paper. It has too often been assumed that once the child has attained certain cognitive levels, he will then be in a position to acquire the linguistic structures in which are expressed the new meanings of which he is capable. To a certain extent this is true. But the question of *how* he acquires these new forms is left unanswered. We have already seen that theories of an associationistic type are inadequate and indeed that children do not just copy the language they hear about them. A child cognitively able to appreciate various types of negation does not by that process simply begin to produce the adult-like negative structures to which he has been exposed. In other words, one must be wary of the types of over-simplification that represent merely the reintroduction of associationistic theories by the back door.

I have not even mentioned the many important aspects of language acquisition which have been studied by the extension of the definition of language beyond the narrow bounds of language structure *per se*. There have now been a large number of important studies on the acquisition of the semantic and pragmatic components of language and on the development of communicative skills by the child (Bates, 1976; Bloom, 1970; Bowerman, 1973a, 1973b, 1976; Bruner, 1974/5, 1975; Clark, 1973a; Garvey, 1975; Keenan, 1974; Mitchell-Kernan & Ervin-Tripp, 1977; Nelson, 1973; Snow, 1977). Language acquisition no longer means merely the acquisition of syntactic structures — which is where the modern investigation of language acquisition began in the 1950s. Since what is meant by "language" has changed dramatically, it can be said that we now know a great deal more about how children deal with the complete language system. There has indeed been much progress. If by contrast, we ask about progress on understanding the acquisition of language *structure*, then we must admit that language acquisition, so defined, remains a mysterious process.

References

Bates, E. (1976) *Language and Context: The Acquisition of Pragmatics*, Academic Press, New York.

Beilin, H. (1975) *Studies in the Cognitive Basis of Language Development*, Academic Press, New York.

Bellugi-Klima, U. (1969) Language acquisition. Paper presented at the Wenner-Gren Foundation for Anthropological Research in the Symposium on Cognitive Studies and Artificial Intelligence Research, Chicago.

Bever, T. G. (1970) The cognitive basis for linguistic structures, *In*: J. R. Hayes (ed.), *Cognition and the Development of Language*, John Wiley & Sons, New York.

Bever, T. G., Mehler, J. R. and Valian, V. V. (1968) Linguistic capacity of very young children, Mimeographed paper.

Bloom, L. (1970) *Language Development: Form and Function in Emerging Grammars*, M.I.T. Press, Cambridge, Massachusetts.

Bowerman, M. (1973a) *Early Syntactic Development*, Cambridge University Press, Cambridge.

Bowerman, M. (1973b) Structural relationships in children's utterances: Syntactic or semantic? *In*: T. E. Moore (ed.), *Cognitive Development and the Acquisition of Language*, Academic Press, New York.

Bowerman, M. (1976) Semantic factors in the acquisition of rules for word use and sentence construction, *In*: D. M. Morehead and A. E. Morehead (eds.), *Normal and Deficient Child Language*, University Park Press, Baltimore.

Braine, M. D. S. (1963) On learning the grammatical order of words, *Psychol. Rev.*, **70**, 323–48.

Bresnan, J. (1978) A realistic transformational grammar. *In*: Morris Halle, Joan Bresnan and George A. Miller (eds.), *Linguistic Theory and Psychological Reality*, M.I.T. Press, Cambridge, Massachusetts.

Brown, R. (1968) The development of questions in child speech, *J. of Verb. Learn. Behav.*, **7**, 279–90.

Brown, R. (1973) *A First Language*, Harvard University Press, Cambridge, Massachusetts.

Brown, R. and Bellugi, U. (1964) Three processes in the child's acquisition of syntax, *Harvard Educational Review*, **34**, 133–51.

Brown, R. and Hanlon, C. (1970) Derivational complexity and the order of acquisition in child speech. *In*: J. R. Hayes (ed.), *Cognition and the Development of Language*, John Wiley and Sons, New York.

Bruner, J. S. (1974/75) From communication to language — A psychological perspective. *Cognition*, **3**, 225–87.

Bruner, J. S. (1975) The ontogenesis of speech acts, *J. Child Lang.* **2**, 1–19.

Bruner, J. S., Goodnow, J. J. and Austin, G. A. (1956) *A Study of Thinking*, John Wiley and Sons, New York.

Cazden, C. (1965) Environmental assistance to the child's acquisition of grammar,

Unpublished doctoral dissertation, Harvard University.

Chomsky, N. (1966) *Cartesian Linguistics*, Harper and Row, New York.

Chomsky, N. (1968) *Language and Mind*, Harcourt Brace Jovanovich, New York.

Chomsky, N. (1975) *Reflections of Language*, Pantheon, New York.

Clark, E. V. (1973a) What's in a word? On the child's acquisition of semantics in his first language, *In*: T. E. Moore (ed.), *Cognitive Development and the Acquisition of Language*, Academic Press, New York.

Clark, E. V. (1973b) Non-linguistic strategies and the acquisition of word meanings, *Cognition*, 2, 161–82.

Cromer, R. F. (1974) The development of language and cognition: The cognition hypothesis, *In*: B. Foss (ed.), *New Perspectives in Child Development*, Penguin Books, Harmondsworth, Middlesex.

Cromer, R. F. (1976a) The cognitive hypothesis of language acquisition and its implications for child language deficiency, *In*: D. M. Morehead and A. E. Morehead (eds.), *Normal and Deficient Child Language*, University Park Press, Baltimore, Maryland.

Cromer, R. F. (1976b) Developmental strategies for language, *In*:V. Hamilton and M. D. Vernon (eds.), *The Development of Cognitive processes*. Academic Press, London and New York.

Cromer, R. F., The Bases of Childhood Dysphasia: A Linguistic Approach, *In*: M. Wyke (ed.), *Developmental Dysphasia*, Academic Press, London.

Dewart, M. H. (1975) A psychological investigation of sentence comprehension by children, Unpublished doctoral dissertation, University College, London.

Donaldson, M. and McGarrigle, J. (1974) Some clues to the nature of semantic development, *J. Child. Lang.*, 1, 185–94.

Efron, R. (1963) Temporal perception, aphasia, and déjà vu, *Brain*, 86, 403–24.

Ferreiro, E. and Sinclair, H. (1971) Temporal relations in language, *Int. J. of Psychol.*, 6, 39–47.

Fodor, J. and Garrett, M. (1966) Some reflections on competence and performance. *In*: J. Lyons and R. J. Wales (eds.), *Psycholinguistics papers*, Edinburgh University Press, Edinburgh.

Fodor, J. A. and Garrett, M. (1967) Some syntactic determinants of sentential complexity, *Perception and Psychophysics*, 2, 289–96.

Garvey, C. (1975) Requests and responses in children's speech, *J. Child Lang.*, 2, 41–63.

Graham, N. C. (1968) Short term memory and syntactic structure in educationally subnormal children, *Language and Speech*, 11, 209–19.

Graham, N. C. (1974) Response strategies in the partial comprehension of sentences, *Language and Speech*, 17, 205–21.

Graham, N. C. and Gulliford, R. A. (1968) A psychological approach to the language deficiencies of educationally subnormal children, *Educational Review*, 20, 136–45.

Huttenlocher, J. and Strauss, S. (1968) Comprehension and a statement's relation to the situation it describes, *J. Verb. Learn. Verb. Behav.*, 7, 300–4.

Huttenlocher, J., Eisenberg, K. and Strauss, S. (1968) Comprehension: Relation between perceived actor and logical subject, *J. Verb. Learn. Verb. Behav.*, 7, 527–30.

Jenkins, J. J. and Palermo, D. S. (1964) Mediation processes and the acquisition of linguistic structure, *In*: U. Bellugi and R. Brown (eds.), The acquisition of language, *Monog. Soc. Res. Ch. Dev.*, 29, serial no. 92.

Keenan, E. C. (1974) Conversational competence in children, *J. Child Lang.*, **1**, 163–83.
Lowe, A. D. and Campbell, R. A. (1965) Temporal discrimination in aphasoid and normal children, *J. Speech and Hearing Res.*, **8**, 313–14.
Macnamara, J. (1972) Cognitive basis of language learning in infants, *Psychol. Rev.*, **79**, 1–13.
McMahon, L. E. (1963) Grammatical analysis as part of understanding a sentence, Unpublished doctoral dissertation, Harvard University.
McNeill, D. (1970a) *The Acquisition of Language*, Harper and Row, New York.
McNeill, D. (1970b) The development of language, *In*: P. H. Mussen (ed.), *Carmichael's Manual of Child Psychology*, Volume 1. John Wiley and Sons, New York.
Mehler, J. (1963) Some effects of grammatical transformations on the recall of English sentences, *J. Verb. Learn. Verb. Behav.*, **2**, 250–62.
Menyuk, P. (1964) Comparison of grammar of children with functionally deviant and normal speech, *J. Speech and Hearing Res.*, **7**, 109–21.
Menyuk, P. (1969) *Sentences Children Use*, M.I.T. Press, Cambridge, Massachusetts.
Miller, G. A. (1964) The psycholinguists, *Encounter*, July, **23**, 29–37.
Miller, G. A. and Chomsky, N. (1963) Finitary models of language users, *In*: R. D. Luce, R. R. Bush and E. Galanter (eds.), *Handbook of Mathematical Psychology* (**Vol. II**), John Wiley and Sons, New York.
Miller, G. A. and McKean, K. C. (1964) A chronometric study of some relations between sentences, *Quart. J. Exp. Psychol.*, **16**, 297–308.
Mitchell-Kernan, C. and Ervin-Tripp, S. (eds.), (1977) *Child Discourse*, Academic Press, New York.
Nelson, K. (1973) Structure and strategy in learning to talk, *Monog. Soc. Res. Chi. Dev.*, **38**, nos. 1–2, serial no. 149.
Ricks, D. M. (1972) The beginnings of vocal communication in infants and autistic children, Unpublished doctorate of medicine thesis, University of London.
Savin, H. B. and Perchonock, E. (1965) Grammatical structure and the immediate recall of English sentences, *J. Verb. Learn. Verb. Behav.*, **4**, 348–53.
Sheldon, A. (1974) The role of parallel function in the acquisition of relative clauses in English, *J. Verb. Learn. Verb. Behav.*, **13**, 272–81.
Sinclair-de-Zwart, H. (1969) Developmental psycholinguistics, *In*: D. Elkind and J. H. Flavell (eds.), *Studies in Cognitive Development*, Oxford University Press, New York.
Sinclair, H. (1971) Sensorimotor action patterns as a condition for the acquisition of syntax, *In*: R. Huxley and E. Ingram (eds.), *Language Acquisition: Models and Methods*, Academic Press, London and New York.
Skinner, B. F. (1957) *Verbal Behavior*, Appleton-Century-Crofts Inc. New York.
Slobin, D. I. (1966) Grammatical Transformations and sentence comprehension in childhood and adulthood, *J. Verb. Learn. Verb. Behav.*, **5**, 219–27.
Slobin, D. I. (1968) Recall of full and truncated passive sentences in connected discourse, *J. Verb. Learn. Verb. Behav.*, **7**, 876–81.
Snow, C. E. (1977) The development of conversation between mothers and babies, *J. Ch. Lang.*, **4**, 1–22.
Strohner, H. and Nelson, K. E. (1974) The young child's development of sentence comprehension: Influence of event probability, nonverbal context, syntactic form, and strategies, *Ch. Dev.*, **45**, 567–76.
Tallal, P. and Piercy, M. (1973a) Defects of non-verbal auditory perception in children with developmental aphasia, *Nature*, Feb. 16, **241**, 468–69.

Tallal, P. and Piercy, M. (1973b) Developmental aphasia: Impaired rate of non-verbal processing as a function of sensory modality, *Neuropsychologia*, 11, 389–98.

Tallal, P. and Piercy, M. (1974) Developmental aphasia: Rate of auditory processing and selective impairment of consonant perception, *Neuropsychologia*, 12, 83–93.

Tallal, P. and Piercy, M. (1975) Developmental aphasia: The perception of brief vowels and extended stop consonants, *Neuropsychologia*, 13, 69–74.

Watt, W. C. (1970) On two hypotheses concerning psycholinguistics. *In*: J. R. Hayes (ed.), *Cognition and the Development of Language*, John Wiley and Sons, New York.

CHAPTER 2

Language Management, Socio-economic Status and Educational Progress

W. P. ROBINSON

School of Education, University of Bristol

Socio-economic Status, Language Use and Educational Progress

Many of the demonstrated and demonstrable correlational links between socio-economic status (SES) and academic achievement have only indirect, insignificant, or irrelevant associations with the language mastery of pupils. Solving the language problems, however these are construed, would not lead to the elimination of all the other socially-based inequalities in educational opportunities. Neither can the language problems themselves be solved without prior or simultaneous changes in the values of many other factors. We need to hold these reservations constantly in mind, not only because they are true but because they are so easily forgotten; at times in the last two decades discussions have been conducted as though language and its mastery was all that was relevant to the equitable distribution of educational resources and opportunities.

From an international perspective the consequences of malnutrition, undernutrition, and hunger might rank as the single set of factors whose removal would lead to the greatest educational benefit to the greatest number of children; and yet one finds examples of "language programmes" being instituted to boost achievement of some of the most seriously undernourished children in the world. Even on the more parochial national scene we have managed to mount language programmes and to ignore rather than remedy some of the more

23

expensive financial implications of the Plowden Report (Central Advisory Council for Education (England), 1967). The analysis of Byrne and Williamson (1971) demonstrating positive associations between per pupil expenditure, SES, and academic achievement has not been taken to a stage where LEAs feel obliged to publish accounts that illustrate an equitable distribution of money around the pupils in their schools. Equality or equity in the provision of material resources is not the only issue. The lists of both school and home background factors associated with variability in educational achievement at primary school are long (see Butler and Kellmer Pringle, Morton-Williams, Peaker, and Wiseman in Central Advisory Council for Education (England), 1967, Vol. 2), and there is no reason to expect the list for secondary achievement to be importantly shorter (see Morton-Williams and Finch, 1968). With such an array of other sources of inequality, it is perhaps strange that differential master of language should have assumed the front centre of the stage.

It has been suggested that this eminence was gained only because there was a dearth of contemporary explanation and justification for the under-achievement of low SES pupils, and that Bernstein's hypotheses about "restricted" and "elaborated" codes became publicly available to fill the hiatus (Bernstein, 1961; 1971 for collected papers). Whether or not this is the case, confinement to a "restricted code" of language use and associated hypotheses became legitimised with indecent alacrity as explanations for the low achievement of low SES children in the minds of many educators; possibilities came to be treated as established facts with irresponsible indifference to the evidence.

And now that the evidence available should oblige us to abandon the thesis, both academics and practitioners hang on; they would rather cling to a mythical raft than start swimming. One can lead an audience through arguments to show that: there is no sociolinguistic definition of "code" that can be operationalised with worthwhile precision, that inconsistencies are common in the more general thesis that developed, that *none* of the relationships postulated between confinement to a "restricted" code and the alleged psychological consequences have been tested and shown to be true, and that the picture offered is in any case partial and incomplete (see Edwards, 1976; Robinson, 1978;

Rosen, 1972), and still members of that audience will insist there is an important core of truth in the story of the "codes". One can ask them to display or cite just one person confined to a restricted code (and 29 per cent of the population are supposed to enjoy that condition), and this is treated as an improper demand. One can ask for examples of discourse indicative of confinement to "restricted code"; most commonly offerings are examples of non-Standard English grammar. But still they cling to the idea that (lower) working class children are trapped by this code. It is as though believers are waiting to find another over-simplified thesis to explain the "facts" before they can escape from their present confinement. Unfortunately until they apprehend these facts they will not be able to comprehend them.

This is not to deny the heuristic value of what was a bold and imaginative suggestion. One healthy consequence of the publication of the Bernstein thesis was that considerable evidence has been amassed about SES differences (and similarities) in language use. One unhealthy consequence is that we have been distracted from an examination both of non-linguistic factors associated with the low achievement of low SES pupils and of the linguistic factors other than those interpreted as relevant to Bernstein's code differences, as I will endeavour to illustrate.

First we contrast the two main views about educational achievement of low SES and language use — the "deficit" and the "difference" view. I will then argue that both positions fail to notice the more basic problem that education is set up as an interindividual competition. This argument will be supported by a brief analysis of the school system, and I will note that both researchers and teachers encourage the perpetuation of that conceptual frame of reference.

The enquiry into the realities of the empirical relationships between SES and language will be abbreviated to a suggestion that there are categories of false negative results and of false positives; studies which have been interpreted as showing no differences on inadequate evidence and studies which have shown differences, but which can be interpreted without recourse to claims about differential language mastery. There is also at least one category of "true" positive differences, but it will be argued that the differences actually manifested are neither of sufficient magnitude nor of an appropriate kind to warrant any claim that they represent differences in the "regulative principles of speech" underlying them. It will be suggested that if it makes sense to suggest that differences are greater among teenagers than toddlers, it may be simpler to attribute any such widening gap to experience of school and treatment by teachers rather than to any "coding" differences related to SES. Experience of chronic failure in school will be proposed as a significant variable, and some ways in which the language management of low SES allow teachers to lead such pupils towards "failure" will be suggested. This alternative will not be bold and imaginative, but at least it has several advantages over the Bernstein story; it comprises a clear, internally consistent set of hypotheses that requires but a minimal invention of undocumented assertions and unprobed processes with which to furnish the minds of the participant.

Deficit versus Difference

The suggestion was made, and acted upon, that children of members of disadvantaged social categories, be these defined in terms of social stratification, ethnicity, geography, or combinations of these, were deficient in their mastery of language, *vis-à-vis* non-disadvantaged children. The choice of the word "deficit" was ill-judged. Such a clearly pejorative word to refer to one end of a distribution of skills whose origins were unknown was to invite wrath rather than reason as a response to the idea. It focussed attention upon the children and encouraged reformers to devise remedies that would treat them directly. In the United States the programs of Head Start, Home Start, and Follow Thru' were instituted (Bereiter and Engelmann, 1966; see Hellmuth 1967, 1968, 1970).

Bernstein's original hypothesis was a stronger version of the more general deficit view that had assumed only quantitative differences in skills: his "restricted code" children differed from "elaborated" code children in that "they have learned two different forms of spoken language; the only thing they have in common is that the words are English" (Bernstein, 1961, p. 168). Most, but not all, of the linguistic differences between these codes were expressed in evaluative rather than descriptive terminology and the psychological consequences were expressed similarly: "difficulty in learning to read", "reading and writing . . . slow", "powers of verbal comprehension . . . limited", "grammar and syntax will pass them by", "thinking will tend to be rigid", "curiosity . . . limited" and "reduced motivation to learn" (*op. cit.* pp. 164–5). At no point was it suggested that the statement of these deficiencies needed qualification; for example, "reduced motivation to learn" was offered as a general statement and was not explicitly confined to children in schools designed for middle class children. From his earliest writings Bernstein was also concerned to change schools, curriculum, and teachers' attitudes and behaviour to accommodate to the characteristics of the lower working class children presenting themselves for education, but the confinement to a "restricted code" was never described as anything but a barrier to educational progress. Bernstein saw "deficiencies" in many features of the system, as the development of his thinking shows (Bernstein, 1975); but he clearly included the low SES child's mastery of language and his psychology as two of these levels.

Both varieties of "deficiency" view were denounced, in the first instance, by linguists. In particular, Labov, Baratz and Stewart (see Williams, 1970) demanded that varieties of language be accorded their appropriate linguistic status. Labov in New York (1973) and Shuy and Wolfram in Detroit (1973) made clear that Black English Vernacular was a ruleful, meaningful system arguably ranking as a "dialect" of English. Earlier Labov (1969) had illustrated how situational factors could be responsible for some earlier misleading diagnoses of the language skills of Negro children. Such analyses demonstrated which phonological realisations and grammatical rules were the same in the two dialects and which were different but equivalent. The movement drew attention to the need for teachers to increase their knowledge and appreciation of the nature of varieties of language and to view children's command of language from a perspective other than one that construed difference as deviations below a standard.

While correctly pointing to ways in which "deficit" theorists had underestimated children's capacities, this view did not proceed to note that there can be differential command of any dialect, and that children could still be seen as advanced, average or retarded within this new frame of reference.

Unfortunately neither view can be used to define and solve the problem of educational backwardness.

Deficiencies of "Deficit" and "Difference" Views

More basic questions have to be posed to illustrate the weakness of both approaches. For the "deficit" approach we can ask, "What would be the criteria for evaluating the success of a compensatory educational programme for Group X?" For the "difference" approach we might ask, "What would be the criteria for evaluating the success of any reorganisation of the educational system to meet the needs of Group X?" In both cases one answer presumably could be, "So that members of Group X are no longer distinguishable from members of the dominant sub-culture in respect of life-chances associated with educational opportunities".

In operation within education this might mean a high proportion of Xs staying on longer at school, more Xs taking more advanced examinations, and more Xs entering tertiary institutions. But would that affect the absolute numbers of students enjoying such activities? The short answer is "No". Places in these institutions are rationed by one means or another. Universities have quotas. Departments within universities have quotas. These are fixed at a higher point in the structure of society. Professional and trade organisations also limit the numbers of who achieve their qualifications. Sixth forms are contained. Numbers of candidates passing national examinations are defined proportionately. These propositions being incontrovertibly true in essentials, it follows that more Xs taking places or passing examinations entails that fewer Ys will do so.

A re-distribution of the numbers of Xs and Ys in these institutions might be defended on grounds of fairness and justice, but it would not in itself solve the problem of the Xs and Ys who do not succeed. Education is arranged like steeplechasing; there are few winners and many losers. The success and failure is integral to both systems as they are presently constituted. We can change how many pass and fail by simple administrative actions, but so long as education is construed or implemented as a competition among individuals with rationing of opportunities in the tertiary sector or the occupational structure, the root problems are likely to remain.

The system is used to classify and differentiate. We look and hope for progress from all pupils, but then assess the pupils in terms of individual differences in progress and attainment. The educational thesis to be developed later is that we have too long neglected the extent to which teachers and others think in terms of differences among pupils. In the field of language management in particular, although we have also to examine why pupils might differ in their performance, we have not looked sufficiently at how teachers perceive, respond to and make use of these differences in pupils' speech and writing.

Researchers too have thought in terms of differences, although for other reasons. They have asked in what ways low and middle SES pupils differ in their use of language. They have not asked, "In what ways are they alike and in what ways different?" Why not? At least two reasons can be given, one theoretical and one methodological. Bernstein's theory argued for differences, and in so far as early researchers were constructively trying to see if there was prima facie empirical support for this thesis, then the sensitivity to differences was a proper bias in the initial search. Once any prima facie case had been established however, we had to become more critical and begin to probe possibilities of elminating differences in ways that the thesis would *not* predict. Even had this line been followed, a critical feature of analytic statistics, as conventionally used, would have undermined the endeavour. When comparing the incidence of features manifested in two groups, we can only ask whether the distributions are such as to have been unlikely to come from two populations with the same mean (or whatever value). The rules only permit us to reject null hypotheses. For reasons that are far from clear to me we are not permitted to accept null hypotheses, only to reject them. As D. Satterly (oral communication) correctly points out the reasons are clear. The alternative hypothesis (H_1) is almost always a composite in that it specifies many possible values of the parameter of interest. However, accepting H_0 means accepting a *single* value when you do not have one: which is illogical! Within that set of conventions we cannot conclude that two sets of corpuses or texts are alike in all respects. Consider however, for example, the problem of describing the number of words for which at least one recognised use is known by

7 year-old middle and low SES children; Templin (1957) gave estimates of 29,600 (SD 9,600) and 24,200 (SD 9,500) respectively. This might mean that both groups can recognise any of 20,000 words, with low SES recognising 4,200 unknown to the middle SES and 9,600 the other way round. The 5,400 word advantage is not in fact significantly greater, and most of the words are known to both. Which are we to emphasise, the similarities or the differences? The truth is we should not emphasise either. We should present reality in terms of both similarities and differences and ignore neither. I shall argue that researchers have ignored the similarities.

SES and Differences in Language Management

We could not now review every study conducted short of publishing a voluminous work, and the most useful course of action is probably to summarise the circumstances in which SES differences do not appear, do appear but for non-linguistic reasons, and do appear for linguistic reasons. We can then ask how these latter come to have educational significance.

The data extant have several limitations. Very few studies have collected samples of speech or writing culled from everyday activities. We still do not know what people do with language in the course of their daily lives. We do not know how often they use which units and structures to what ends, when, where and how. Most studies have collected speech or writing in circumscribed contexts defined by the investigators. Many have involved school-like activities in school settings and as such have promoted the study of some functions of language to the exclusion of others. The representational function of language has been the dominant concern (Robinson, 1978). Social functions of regulating the affect and behaviour of self and others appear explicitly in only a few investigations (e.g. Turner, 1973). The work published retains its value and relevance to education within these limitations, but we should not imagine that we are knowledgeable either about SES skills in the many other functions of language yet to be investigated or about the role of language in life as it is lived.

It would be misleading not to note that no SES differences have been reported in a number of studies. Of these a high proportion have suffered from errors of method in sampling, scoring and other aspects of design which vitiate the conclusions drawn (see Robinson, 1979). For example, SES of school rather than child has been used for sampling. Speech variables have been counted on very small corpuses. Some speech variables selected for scoring have been strangely unrelated to any theoretical expectation.

One condition that has generated differences has been that where SES groups *interpret the tasks set differently*. For example, Hawkins (1969) reported that relative to their middle SES peers low SES children more frequently used pronouns and adjuncts such as "here" and "there" without giving further verbal elaboration of the referents of these items. What he does not relate is that the situation was one where pointing could have been used to disambiguate the references. Francis (1974) found no SES differences in this exophoric reference in a situation which she claims was comparable except that non-verbal signalling would have been of no avail.

Activities in school not only require children frequently to tell teachers things already known to the teachers, they also require the adoption of classroom norms that are not made explicit. Williams and Naremore (1969) showed that middle SES children were more likely than low SES children to "elaborate" in reply to a "naming" question such as "Did you watch TV last night?" The linguistic differences disappeared when probes for elaboration were given to the low SES children.

Interestingly enough, in both cases it was the low SES children who were more likely to interpret instructions at face value; the middle SES were the ones who were more likely to know the hidden and implicit assumptions and meanings of the norms of classroomese. When the verbal behaviour of low SES pupils can be modified simply by making instructions explicit, confinement to "restricted code" is clearly too strong an explanation for their initial behaviour.

A second category is similar to the first: *knowing the norms of "good" performance*. Many investigators have asked pupils and students to write essays (Lawton, 1968; Owens, 1976; Poole, 1976; Rushton and Young, 1975). Were they to write good essays or bad essays? What constitutes a "good" essay? And can you actually write a good essay if you want to do so? To come close to being crass in caricature and yet remain correct in essence, we may suggest that for school essays to be defined as good they must at least exhibit variety of structure and lexis and manifest a reasonable incidence of subordination, modification and other forms of linkage and elaboration: occasionally at least, the particular and concrete must be elevated to the general and more abstract. An examination of the coding frames used by researchers will show that those are the very aspects represented as scoring categories in analysis, and an inspection of the results will show that these categories frequently differentiate between the SES groups. But why should middle SES pupils and students differ from their low SES peers in these productions? From elsewhere we know that middle SES students are more likely to inject standards into activities where none are made explicit (Rosen and D'Andrade, 1959; Rosen, 1962) and that this may be particularly likely for academic activities (see Hess, 1970 for a general review of SES differences). That middle SES pupils are more aware of what constitutes good performance in the minds of teachers is as yet no more than a plausible hypothesis. That they are better at generating "good" essays is the evidence of years of English examinations and applications of tests of English attainment. Of the four relevant references cited above, Rushton and Young show that the differences can be reversed when low SES are better educated in the particular activity than middle SES, namely technical writing. While in one sense this is not surprising, it nevertheless renders it improbable that such creatures began to write these essays from a base that was so different that "the only thing . . . in common is that the words are English".

Both of these categories of SES differences appear to stem from differences in knowledge of conventions and practices rather than qualitative differences in orientation to language and to the world. If linguistic differences between groups can be eliminated simply by making task requirements more explicit and precise, then the obvious educational strategy is for teachers to be less ambiguous and presumptive in their requests and instructions, make clear what the rules of the game are, and check that children have understood the situation before they have to speak or write. (How often are children shown a good essay and a bad essay and taken through a reasoned and detailed account of how the differential judgements came to be applied?)

Labov (1969) adds a third category of *pupil's unwillingness to accept the demands of a task*. The logical force of this possibility is incontrovertible. Its empirical force will presumably vary with respondents, tasks, and contexts of situation. The argument might be seen as having only a weak relevance in those investigations where all the respondents cooperate sufficiently for any non-cooperation to be obvious to a scorer or observer. A lesser measure of apparent cooperation by low SES subjects may well account for some of the differences observed, but an assessment of its significance for data already collected is not possible.

Although these three categories of reason for the occurrence of SES differences in speech are relevant to the interests of the sociolinguist, ethnographer of communication, and the psychologist, they are not relevant to the questions of SES differential mastery of the units and structures of language *per se* — and each offers a simpler explanation of observed speech differences than does Bernstein's thesis about codes.

SES differences are also commonly found when the *task demands stretch the proficiency of the children*, and the sample is controlled for age. At any particular age SES differences at one or more levels of linguistic analysis can be demonstrated. Irwin (1948) claimed that middle SES infants articulated distinguishable phonemes earlier than low SES infants, and Templin (1957) reported a continuing lag among low SES for various phonological units through to the age of 5. With 5 year old Canadian children Bruck and Tucker (1974) found low SES children made more phrase structure and more morphological errors than middle SES children on a variety of tasks. Six months later these differences were much attenuated. Transformational errors did not discriminate between the groups at either age. The simplest interpretation is that many grammatical features had been mastered by all the children at the pre-test, and that there is at least some rough sequence of development, and that the middle SES children were ahead. All the time children are still developing their knowledge of English grammar, there will be some features which will show up SES differences; there are many others which would not. The same may well be true of active and passive vocabulary, semantics, and pragmatics. By testing at the leading edge SES differences can be found; testing for the already wholly mastered would yield no differences. From the Bernstein perspective the critical point would be whether the developments are in the same direction. Turner's (1973) analysis of SES differences at ages 5 and 7 in the use of speech for controlling others reveals age and SES differences, but little difference between the 7 year old low SES and the 5 year old middle SES children. (If low SES are behind middle SES, and we label them as "backward" or "deficient", should we not label babies backward and deficient because their command of language is less than that of toddlers? Why are age norms a basis for using evaluative rather than descriptive terms to refer to deviations from these norms? Or is it the case that whatever words we do choose will acquire evaluative connotations within our culture? Yet outside the educational game does it really matter whether a child learns how to use passive verbs at 5 or 6? That he learns eventually may be important, but that he learns before his age peers could be unimportant.)

Are these developmentally related differences in linguistic mastery in fact so great that they are intellectually important? In the SES literature as a whole, the most frequently quoted differences in percentage incidence of features are probably below 10; some are as low as 2. While 34 per cent of sentences containing subordinate clauses may, under certain conditions, be significantly higher than an incidence of 32 per cent statistically speaking, such a gap is unlikely to be associated with or result in substantial differences in communicative efficiency or effectiveness. These results have normally been interpreted as supporting the Bernstein thesis (see Poole, 1976). I suggest that if the differences found are small over *all* levels of linguistic analysis in most studies, this constitutes a refutation of Bernstein's thesis of code differences; the results are more economically interpreted as most members of both SES groups defining tasks in the same way and performing very similarly in them.

The accident of a limitation of methodology associated with analytic statistics and the researchers' failure to notice this might therefore be at least partly responsible for the attention to the differences and the neglect of the similarities. That we have no mathematically defensible way of answering the appropriate questions does not however justify the adoption of a mathematically defensible way of answering the wrong ones. Judgement without numerical warranties of confidence will have to be made. The data are available for inspection and individuals are free to examine them, arrive at their conclusions, and then defend these. My conclusion is that within the limitations of the data so far collected, differences observed result from the factors mentioned here and not from restricted and elaborated codes — others might come to different conclusions. Such conclusions would need supplementary justification in the form of explaining why a difference of this magnitude on this variable should be psychologically as well as statistically significant.

While many of the differences observed in younger children will cease to exist as they mature, there are three points to which we should give consideration, each of which can act to maintain or increase the extent of differences. Low SES pupils leave the educational system earlier than middle SES pupils. Someone who passes through to a higher degree in university will have spent 20 years as an academic learner compared with 10 years for the 15 year old leaver. For the former, the second 10 years is spent with an adult brain at his service. Those who enter occupations where powers of verbal expression are exercised *in extenso* on a daily basis will be under more pressure to develop language skills than someone driving a train. Age of leaving education is sharply differentiated by SES of origin as is the occupation of non-manual jobs. Low SES will therefore suffer from a residual lag at the time they leave school and, in so far as both the subsequent opportunities and demands made upon the middle SES increase their language management skills, the gap between them and their low SES age peers will widen. (Low SES may also be increasing their language management skills within their environments; at present we remain ignorant about their adult usage.)

It will also be true that in so far as middle and low SES children are being socialised into groups and subcultures with different registers and dialects there will be divergence. If there is greater commonality between school language and home language for one group than the other, this will enhance within school differences. While it is usually assumed that the speech of middle class homes is like that of school, no-one has yet advanced any evidence about such speech that shows this to be so. The only extant analysis of conversations in an extended middle SES family revealed a structure and content that looked remarkably like some of the characteristics Bernstein attributed to *restricted code* speech: considerable predictability, with most apparent information being already known to the listener, a high incidence of utterances serving social rather than representational functions etc. (Phillips, 1973). Wells (1977) reports little use of the tutorial (instructional) function of speech even between mother and child, regardless of SES. Certainly mothers do not follow Flanders' well-documented rule of two thirds: in American classrooms two thirds of the time involves talking, of which two thirds is teacher talk of which two thirds is lecturing (see Dunkin and Biddle, 1974). What does it mean to say the speech of the school is like the speech of the middle SES home? Even if middle SES speech is "more similar" to school language, this may once more be an example of some difference with much similarity. At the level of grammar, for example, "dialectical" differences between Black English Vernacular and Standard American English are represented by fewer than 50 rules (Labov, 1973; Shuy and Wolfram, 1973), similarities by many more than 50; presumably low SES British dialects would involve a comparable number of similarities and differences.

The third reason may affect norms relevant to the verbal repertoire children are prepared to develop. If pupils come to reject school, they will reject the speech and writing that school values. Very large numbers of pupils, particularly those of low SES, are indifferent to or hostile towards much of secondary school activity (Morton-Williams and Finch, 1968; Robinson, 1975). The "boredom" cycle I proposed as a vehicle for developing and maintaining a depressed level of interest and performance was particularly applicable to low SES pupils. One factor of importance in this system was failure. Many low SES children experience biographies of protracted failure for most of their school lives. This may be one critical linking factor.

What constitutes failure in school? As yet we do not know which pupils come to see themselves as failures and why. Neither do we know the extent to which teachers transmit such ideas to the pupils in their charge. For the argument presented here we have to rely on objective indices of failure, and hope that they are strongly correlated with perceived failure. It may be that most of the pupils who come to see themselves as failures begin with a history of backwardness, and it is worth reminding ourselves how children become backward or below average. We construct tests of ability or achievement designed to distribute children of a particular age group about a norm, and are then surprised at the number who make scores below that norm. The concept of a "backward" reader is our invention and definition, and it is totally inappropriate to ask why the general incidence of backward readers is what it is. Clearly testing can be used constructively as is the case with assessment that is used as a basis of information for extending specially designed educative measures. Diagnostic testing associated with prophylactic action is to be sharply distinguished from rank-ordering that is primarily classificatory.

If classificatory activities are endemic in education, then perhaps we should look at the consequences of prolonged experience of unfavourable comparisons for insight into the problems of the unsuccessful, and examine ways in which the language management of low SES pupils might put them in particular at risk in these processes.

SES, Language Management and the Reactions of Teachers

Since even the brief abbreviated argument to be set out here has a number of stages, it may be more easily apprehended if set out in propositional form. The generalisations made should be seen as statistical not universal; "teachers" does *not* mean all teachers at all times — it means a sufficient number of teachers on a sufficient number of occasions for the proposition presented to be more likely to be true than the opposite of the proposition. Readers familiar with the "self-fulfilling prophecy" (see Good and Brophy, 1974 for a detailed review of its nature and current status) will detect the indebtedness to them. Readers are less likely to be familiar with Tajfel and Turner's theory of intergroup relations from which other concepts and ideas are drawn (see Tajfel (1978) or Tajfel and Turner (1979), for a summary and below Proposition 6).

(1). *Teachers perceive children in terms of individual differences predictive of eventual academic success and failure.*

(1a). *The language management of children is one set of factors used for this discrimination.*

Hargreaves (1977) reviews evidence and theory relevant to teacher's perceptions of pupils. We can begin to see how the research thinking about teachers' thinking is maturing. While recognising the special weight attached to first impressions of pupils, we now recognise that these may be no more than the weakest of categorisations serving as a point of departure for interaction. Impressions can change not only in content but form. First concerns may be focussed on global goodness as a pupil; later analysis may be broadened and differentiated into concern for a complicated person. Behaviour of pupils may come to be seen as interactions of situational factors and personality predispositions rather than as immutable inevitabilities of fixed traits. This looser model that recognises variability across time, situations, and teachers remains an observer's account, and is still not an account of a participant's behaviour. How far our behaviour is informed and controlled by what we *say* about people is another source of variability. (Psychiatrists in one-to-one or one-to-few relationships may be expected to move towards such refinements faster than teachers for whom the face-to-face context is one-to-many, and whose contacts are of specified duration and content.)

In spite of this it seems that initial judgements can be made and are made; speech can be a significant determinant of these (1a). Seligman, Tucker and Lambert (1972) compared the ways in which examples of written work and drawing, photographs, and samples of speech controlled for content affected student teachers' judgements about "good student" (academically), privilege, intelligence, enthusiasm, self-confidence and gentleness. Speech differentiated on all six characteristics, compositions and drawings and face on three each; speech varying only in phonological and paralinguistic features. Eltis (1978) obtained comparable results with Australian student teachers, but found that graduate teachers with at least three years' experience placed less weight on voice and more on composition. His rating scales included one predicting academic success. The extent to which these beliefs and inferences are valid remains in doubt. While some authors write as though predictions of failure from "disadvantaged" speech are attributable to invalid assumptions by teachers (Edwards, J.R., in press), and Eltis showed that allocation to streams of owners of voices whose IQs were known exaggerated the observed correlation between IQs and voice characteristics, evidence for a measure of validity in the inference has some strength. Frender, Brown and Lambert (1972) have shown that the speech of low achievers differs from that of high achievers in ways that are consistently in the same direction as teachers' judgements. Williams (1976) extended the inferential studies to show how other subject and teacher variables complicate the judgements but leave the basic findings as before. A succession of American studies (see Robinson, 1979 for a bibliography) have yielded very high accuracy of identification of SES from speech samples lasting less than half a minute.

Both propositions are reasonably established, and the second can be extended to say that teachers can and do discriminate in terms of background variables such as SES, psychological variables such as intelligence, reliability, trustworthiness etc. and link both predictively to likely success as a pupil. While there are positive *correlations* among these variables, which may be constructed into explanations linking the three, the present situation is one where it is plausible to suggest that:

(1) many teachers overestimate the size of the real correlations between SES, speech, and academic potential;

(2) both teachers and researchers may misinterpret the nature of these links; on currently available evidence these might just as well be explained as consequences of the discriminatory behaviour of teachers as reasons for differences in student achievement.

(2). *The differentials are communicated to and perceived by children*
In a case study Rist (1970) found entering kindergarten children were quickly stratified into three groups, mainly on the basis of SES. The groups were treated differently, and while still in kindergarten, the children accepted this classification and treated each other accordingly. Both Barker Lunn (1970) and Ferri (1972) related teacher judgements of pupils positively to self images of those pupils. Palfrey (1973) contrasted self concepts of fourth year secondary pupils from adjoining schools, attributing differences indirectly to the strangely opposed beliefs of their respective Head teachers. Such evidence that

exists points to children generally accepting as well as appreciating teachers' views of them.

(3).   *Teachers distribute both the quantity and quality of interactions with children unevenly.*

(3a).   *While the values guiding this distribution can vary from teacher to teacher (and within a teacher from context to context), at present the dominant principle of such rationing is "To him that hath shall be given, and he that hath not, from him shall be taken away even that which he hath".*

The general proposition has an inevitability about its truth that its corollary has not. Rosenthal and Jacobson's (1965) original promotion of the self-fulfilling prophecy assumed that such principles and practices were mediating between teacher expectations and student achievement, but did not actually watch how teachers interacted with pupils. Subsequent relevant studies have been comprehensively reviewed by Brophy and Good (1974) and Elashoff and Snow (1971). The kinds of differences found are mentioned under Proposition 4, and, with one exception, have been consistent with the corollary as worded. When investigating possibilities of the influence of expectancy effects among mentally retarded children, Anderson and Rosenthal (1968) found that teachers spent most time with the most retarded. The question is an empirical one. In order to move to more specific predictive possibilities it would be necessary to know a teacher's values and theories of teaching, in addition to estimating those demand characteristics of pupils which might limit the realisation of possibilities in particular contexts.

(4).   *Differential treatment by teachers is relevant to the quality and quantity of pupils' development*

Some extensive reviews of the literature remain relatively agnostic (Dunkin and Biddle, 1974) about the generalisations to be made about the process variables relevant to pupil progress. A full consideration of the complexities militates in this direction, but if parameters are set down that restrict the generalisation to the mythical average child, the list of variables specified by Brophy and Good (1974) points to what kinds of procedures are likely to facilitate learning, given the cultural context concerned: frequency of contact initiated by teacher (e.g. questions asked), frequency of contact with teacher involving praise and absence of such contact involving criticism of either work or behaviour, teacher pausing longer for answers and re-phrasing questions, frequency of procedural and work-related contacts initiated by the child, absence of answers evoking no evaluating reaction, absence of wrong answers or reading problems not followed by teacher repetition or re-phrasing. These can readily be conceived as a higher incidence of learning opportunities in a more supportive context.

(5). *In the absence of opposing views, children's own comparisons and self-perception will come to agree with those of their teachers*

    (5a). *While those comparisons may be quantitative and malleable in the early years of schooling, through time, ceteris paribus, they are likely to become categorical and stable*

    (5b). *For many children this categorisation will define them as academic "failures"*

    (5c). *Low SES children are particularly likely to see themselves as failures*

Rist (1970) may again be quoted to illustrate the earliness of onset with which such comparisons can appear in the thinking and behaviour of children. Hargreaves (1967) has demonstrated the operation of strong categorisation in the secondary careers of boys. The members of the C and D streams in the secondary modern school he studied were clear in their identification with the peer group of the academically unsuccessful. Their view of their academic status and other attributes corresponded to those of the teachers and their A stream peers. The A stream were equally confident of their identity.

Although Hargreaves was writing about a predominantly working class school, what he brings alive there is implicit in the internationally collected statistics (Husen, 1972) and in those of England and Wales (Central Advisory Council for Education, 1967; Douglas, 1964; Douglas, Ross and Simpson, 1971; Kellmer Pringle, Butler and Davie, 1966; Morton Williams and Finch, 1968). Whether the objective reality of low SES educational failure is perceived as such by the pupils concerned has not been a focus of attention. American work on low self-esteem and "negative self-concepts" (see Brookover, 1969; Coopersmith, 1967; Purkey, 1970) does however integrate this perception with poor academic performance and teacher judgements. Brookover and others have demonstrated circumstances under which self-esteem can be raised and shown to enhance school performance. What options are open to the chronically insulted and debased?

(6).   *Chronic exposure to experiences that reduce self-esteem will lead to attempts to repair this negative personal or social identity. The dimensions of value to any repaired identity will be either independent of or antagonistic to those academic and social values used to define pupils as failures*

The Tajfel-Turner (1979) theory of intergroup relations can be used to generate a number of expectations. The theory is intended to explain the behaviour of individuals not qua individuals but qua members of social groups. If persons categorise themselves as members of a social group, they will compare the attributes of the group with those of others. A basic assumption is that individuals strive to achieve and/or maintain a positive social identity. This positive social identity is based on being able to make favourable comparisons between in-group and some relevant out-groups. If the social identity is not acceptable, individuals will strive either to leave their existing group for a preferable one or to enhance the value of their existing group. What are the implications for the language of the classroom? Where classrooms contain a sufficient strength of failed pupils, one would expect classroom interaction to lose its academic thrust. Regardless of whether teachers of such classes persist with the pursuit of school objectives or conspire and connive at a *modus vivendi*, the classroom interaction is likely to manifest symptoms of subversion or conversion into larking about and pushing the teacher. High esteem will derive from proficiency and daringness in this subversion and will be supported by peers, which is exactly what Hargreaves (1967) demonstrated. What else, other than apathy (Robinson, 1975) could be expected? Poole and Jones (1977) found that 55 per cent of their sample of "early leavers" mentioned boredom or failure as a major reason for their departure.

The language management of such pupils would be expected to take on those characteristics cited by Bernstein as indicative of a restricted code: speech should serve predominantly social functions of testing authority, outwitting authority and joking. Features of language associated with school should be rejected. This should extend to a rejection of accents and grammar associated with the dialect of

Standard English and the adoption of low SES dialect, elaborated with adolescent specialities. In this account the restricted code emerges as a consequence of experience in school, not a cause of it; it emerges as an important factor establishing a social identity of positive value to its owner and his peers.

The route to these conclusions has been long. It may have appeared to lose language in its intermediate stages, but this is appearance only. The importance of the speech and writing of pupils as a basis for teachers' judgements continues in its relevance through the processes described, as its re-emergence at the final stage implies.

There is no denial that the knowledge of language and the structures of speech codes may be relevant to psychological processes of perception, thinking, learning, remembering and communicating. We should note however that the currently available evidence gives no warrant nor necessity for the invocation of such hypotheses to explain the presently appearing SES differentials in educational performance.

Conclusions

If it is the case that the emphasis placed here is justified and that inferences of teachers based in part upon the speech and writing of pupils are a significant source of discriminatory judgement and subsequent teaching, there are a number of cosmetic possibilities for genuine but superficial improvement.

We can ask teachers to increase their knowledge and understanding of what language is and how it works. Hopefully, more will come to appreciate there is not a single Standard English with its Received Pronunciation; that there is no single system to which everyone aspires or conforms regardless of situation, participants, modes, and other variables of context. A wider appreciation of the realities rather than the myths of language management should lead to modifications of the treatment of pupils that would improve upon the present state of affairs. We might also ask teachers to examine the validity of belief systems that underpin their assessments of pupils' potential; particularly their inferences from speech and writing? Do they enable unwarranted predictions about individual pupils to come true? Is their treatment of a response or initiatives of a pupil one that maximises the learning possibilities or is it predicated on an assumption that this pupil is a non-learner? To ask teachers to examine the quality and quantity of their interactions to see whether these accord with what they would consider to be fair is to ask much. To ask them to try to prevent pupils from coming to see themselves as "failures" does not seem to be asking so much.

Given that the inter-individual competitiveness of education in our society will not disappear in the immediate future, we can nevertheless take steps to represent that competition differently. The theory of inter-group relations, as did reference group theory, would stress that the evaluative framework within which an individual operates is mutable. In sporting activities many people enjoy competing within their own ability category. They do not spend each game regretting that they are not of Olympic standard; it does not matter that they are not. Typically no-one labels them as "deficient" against any criterion, and neither are they seen as "failed" people or members of society. In so far as pupils can identify themselves as members of categories with positively valued characteristics consistent with educational development all is well. It may be that the proliferation of examinations at secondary level has helped in this regard, as have the successful efforts of teachers to integrate pupils within their schools and groupings within the schools.

Moves to stress the importance of progress (intra-individual competition) that confront individuals with what they can now do but could not manage before are another means of encouraging further development and the maintenance of self-esteem. The same is true of emphasis upon mastery *per se*, the sense of satisfaction to be derived from control of the environment. Progress towards the implementation of these last two policies would be more than cosmetic.

References

Anderson, D. and Rosenthal, R. (1968) Some effects of interpersonal expectancy and social interaction on institutionalised retarded children, *Proceedings of the 76th Annual Convention of the American Psychological Association*, 3, 479–80.

Barker-Lunn, J. C. (1970) *Streaming in the Primary School*, National Foundation for Educational Research, Slough.

Bereiter, C. and Engelmann, S. (1966) *Teaching Disadvantaged Children in the Pre-School*, Prentice Hall, New Jersey.

Bernstein, B. (1961) Social structure, language, and learning, *Educational Research*, **3**, 163–76.

Bernstein, B. (1971) *Class, Codes and Contexts: Vol. I Theoretical Studies Towards a Sociology of Language*, Routledge, London.

Bernstein, B. (1975) *Class, Codes and Control*, Vol. 3, Routledge, London.

Brookover, W. B. (1969) *Self Concept and Achievement*, paper presented to American Educational Research Association, Los Angeles.

Brophy, J.E. and Good, T. L. (1974) *Teacher-Student Relationships*, Holt, New York.

Bruck, M. and Tucker, W. (1974) Social class differences in the acquisition of school language, *Merrill Palmer Quarterly*, **20**, 205–20.

Byrne, D. S. and Williamson, W. (1971) The myth of the restricted code, *No. 1, Working Papers in Sociology*, University of Durham.

Central Advisory Council for Education (England) (1967) *Children and their Primary Schools*, Vols. 1 and 2, H.M.S.O., London.

Coopersmith, S. (1967) *The Antecedents of Self-esteem*, Freeman, San Francisco.

Douglas, J. W. B. (1964) *The Home and the School*, MacGibbon and Kee, London.

Douglas, J. W. B. Ross, J. M. and Simpson, H. P. (1971) *All our Future,* Panther, London.

Dunkin, M. J. and Biddle, B. J. (1974) *The Study of Teaching*, Holt. New York.

Edwards, A. D. (1976) *Language in Culture and Class*, Heinemann, London.

Edwards, J. R. Judgements and competence in the reactions to disadvantaged speech, *In*: R. N. St. Clair and H. Giles (eds.), (in press) *Language and Social Psychology*, Blackwell, Oxford.

Elashoff, J. and Snow, R. (1971) *Pygmalion Re-considered*, Charles A. Jones, Ohio.

Eltis, K. (1978) *The Ascription of Attributes to Pupils by Teachers and Student Teachers with Particular Reference to the Influence of Voice in this Process*, Sydney, Macquarie University, Ph.D. Thesis.

Fasold, R. W. and Wolfram, W. (1973) Some linguistic features of negro dialect, *In*: J. S. de Stefano (ed.), *Language, Society and Education*, Worthington, Ohio, Charles A. Jones, Ohio.

Ferrie, E. (1972) *Streaming: Two Years Later*, National Foundation for Educational Research, Slough.

Francis, H. (1974), Social Class, Reference and Context, *Language and Speech*, **17**, 193–98.

Frender, R., Brown, B. L. and Lambert, W. E. (1970) The role of speech characteristics in scholastic success, *Canad. J. Behav. Sci.,* **2**, 299–306.

Frender, R. and Lambert, W. E. (1972) Speech style and scholastic success: the tentative relationships and possible implications for lower class children, *Monograph Series on Language and Linguistics*, **25**, 237–71.

Hargreaves, D. H. (1967) *Social Relations in a Secondary School*, Routledge, London.

Hargreaves, D. H. (1977) The process of typification in classroom interactions models and methods, *Bri. J. Ed. Psychol.*, **47**, 274–84.

Hawkins, P. R. (1969) Social class, the nominal group, and preference, *Lang. and Speech*, **12**, 125–55.

Hellmuth, J. (1967, 1968, 1970) *The Disadvantaged Child,* Vols. 1, 2, and 3, Brunner-Mazel, New York.

Hess, R. D. (1970) Social class and ethnic influence on socialisation, *In*: P. H. Mussen (ed.), *Carmichael's Manual of Child Psychology*, Wiley, New York.

Husen, T. (1972) *Social Background and Educational Career*, OECD, Paris.

Irwin, O. C. (1948) Infant speech: the effect of family occupational status and of age on sound frequency, *J. Sp. Hear. Dis.*, **13**, 320–23.

Kellmer-Pringle, M. L., Butler, N. R. and Davie, B. (1966) *11,000 Seven-Year-Olds*, Longmans, London.

Labov, W. (1969) The logic of non-standard English, *Georgetown Monogr., Language and Linguistics*, **22**, 1–31.

Labov, W. and Cohen, P. (1973) Systematic relations of standard and non-standard rules in the grammars of negro speakers, *In*: J. S. de Stefano (ed.), *Language, Society and Education*, Charles A. Jones, Ohio.

Lawton, D. (1968) *Social Class, Language and Education*, Routledge, London.

Morton-Williams, R. and Finch, S. (1968) *Young School Leavers*, H.M.S.O., London.

Nash, R. (1976) *Teacher Expectations and Pupil Learning*, Routledge, London.

Owens, L. C. (1976) Syntax in children's written composition, socioeconomic status, and cognitive development, *Aust. J. Ed.*, **20**, 202–22.

Palfrey, C. F. (1973) Headteachers' expectations and their pupils' self-concepts, *Educational Research*, **16**, 123–27.

Phillips, D. J. (1973) How an Australian family communicates, *Linguistic Communications*, **10**, 73–107.

Poole, M. E. (1976) *Social Class and Language and Utilisation at the Tertiary Level*, University of Queensland Press, Brisbane.

Poole, M. E. and Jones, D. (1977) *Early School Leavers*, La Trobe, Melbourne, La Trobe 15 to 18 year old Project.

Purkey, W. W. (1970) *Self Concept and School Achievement*, Englewood Cliffs, N.J., Prentice Hall, New Jersey.

Rist, R. (1970) Student social class and teacher expectations: the self-fulfilling prophecy in ghetto education, *Harvard Education Review*, **40**, 411–51.

Robinson, W. P. (1975) Boredom at school, *Br. J. Educ. Psychol.*, **45**, 141–52.

Robinson, W. P. (1978) *Language Management in Education: the Australian Context*, Allen & Unwin, Sydney.

Robinson, W. P. (1979) Speech markers and socio-economic status, *In*: H. Giles and K. Scherer (eds.), *Social Markers in Speech*, Cambridge University Press, Cambridge.

Rosen, B. C. and D'Andrade, R. C. (1959) The psycho-social origins of achievement motivation, *Sociometry*, **22**, 185–218.

Rosen, B. C. (1962) Socialisation and Achievement Motivation in Brazil, *American Sociological Review*, **27**, 612–24.

Rosen, H. (1972) *Language and Class: A Critical Look at the Theories of Basil Bernstein*, Falling Wall Press, Bristol.

Rosenthal, R. and Jacobson, L. (1968) *Pygmalion in the Classroom*, Holt, New York.

Rushton, J. and Young, G. (1975) Context and complexity in working-class language, *Language and Speech*, **18**, 366–87.

Seligman, C. R., Tucker, G. R. and Lambert, W. E. (1972) The effects of speech style and other attributes on teachers' attitudes towards pupils, *Language in Society*, **1**, 131–42.

Shuy, R. W. and Wolfram, W. A. (1973) Chapter in: J. S. de Stefano (ed.), *Language and Education*, Charles A. Jones, Ohio.

de Stefano, J. S. (ed.) (1973) *Language, Society and Education*, Charles A. Jones, Ohio.

Tajfel, H. (1978) *Differentiation between Social Groups*, Academic Press, London.

Tajfel, H. and Turner, J. (1979) An integrative theory of intergroup conflict, *In*: W. G. Austin and S. Worchel (eds.), *The Social Psychology of Intergroup Relations*, Brooks Cole, California.

Templin, M. C. (1957) *Certain Language Skills in Children*, University of Minnesota Press, Minneapolis.

Turner. G. J. (1973) Social class and children's language of control at ages five and seven, *In*: B. Bernstein (ed.), *Class, Codes, and Control*, Vol. 2, Routledge, London.

Wells, C. G. (1977) Language use and educational success, *Research in Education*, **18**, 9–34.

Williams, F. (ed.) (1970) *Language and Poverty*, Chicago, Markham, Chicago.

Williams, F. and Naremore, R. C. (1969) On the functional analysis of social class differences in modes of speech, *Speech Monographs*, **36**, 77–102.

Williams, F. H. (ed.) (1976) *Explorations of the Linguistic Attitudes of Teachers*, Newbury House, Mass.

CHAPTER 3

Four Year Olds Talking to Mothers and Teachers

BARBARA TIZARD, HELEN CARMICHAEL, MARTIN HUGHES
and GILL PINKERTON

Thomas Coram Research Unit, London

Introduction

Since the sixties, people professionally concerned with young children
— e.g. teachers and doctors — have focussed a good deal of attention
on their language needs. This has been especially true in Britain and
the United States. Most of this discussion has centred not on basic
developmental issues, e.g. the role of language in thinking, or the
processes by which language is acquired, but on the origins of educational failure — that is, the inadequacy of working-class children's
language, and the presumed relationship between this language deficit
and educational difficulties.

If educational difficulties are caused by inadequate language experience at home the implication seems clear — what we should do is
attempt to influence the way in which working-class parents talk to
their young children, e.g. by the use of specially trained health visitors,
or educational visitors, by talks at clinics etc., and as a back-up get
these children into nursery schools as soon as possible, so that they can
be exposed to compensatory language experiences. Both these policies
were advocated in the recent Bullock report, (Bullock, 1975) which
suggested that health visitors should urge parents to "bathe their
children in language", whilst the skills and knowledge of the nursery
and infant teacher should be used to give "measured attention to the
children's language needs".

This two-prong policy rests on a number of highly questionable assumptions. Firstly, it assumes that we understand the processes of language development and the effect of different kind of interventions on it. This is, of course, far from the case: we know quite a lot about the *stages* in language acquisition, but very little about the kinds of experience which facilitate the development in the child of various aspects of language. *Should* a child be "bathed in language", and if he were, what would be the effect on his language development? Or should we not also consider the effect on his language development of having a wide range of experiences or a wide range of people to talk to?

The second assumption is that the day-to-day language interactions of parents and children can be effectively altered by advice about how to talk. We have, for example, heard a teacher urge a group of mothers to "use more open-ended questions" when talking to their children. But how and why parents talk to their children is the resultant of many complex factors, notably status relationships within the family, and also what seems to them important to communicate. This in turn is likely to depend on a whole set of underlying attitudes, including their belief about what the children are going to need to function effectively in society. Quite aside, then, from the question of whether it is wise to make people self-conscious about the way they talk to their children, it seems likely that intervention at this superficial level will be ineffective.

The third assumption on which current educational interventions are based is that the language used in working-class homes is markedly inadequate. This is an article of faith for many, perhaps for most, teachers – we have all of us heard the school failure of a particular child, or of a social class or even an ethnic group, explained as due to the supposed fact that "no-one speaks to him at home" or that "the language in his home is very poor".

Whilst this is no doubt true in some cases, the belief that school difficulties are due to inadequate language experience at home is based on remarkably little firm evidence of what language usage in different homes is actually like. In fact, statements about working-class language at home are usually not much more than guesses, made respectable by references to misunderstood and over-simplified versions of Bernstein's theories. Only in the last few years have attempts been made in Britain, notably by Wootton in Aberdeen (Wootton, 1974), and Wells in Bristol (Wells, 1975), to record spontaneous parent-child talk in a variety of homes; the findings of these studies do not support the cruder theories about working-class language inadequacy.

The final widely held assumption is that nursery and infant teachers, because of their special training, are in fact likely to be especially successful at promoting language development. In recent interviews with nursery school staff (Tizard, 1978) we found that in working- class areas all the teachers believed that the children's main gain from school attendance was "improved language". Yet, there is considerable research evidence that attendance at an ordinary nursery school makes no difference to children's language development (Tizard, 1975).

One explanation for the teacher's belief to the contrary is clear – it derives from the fact that she *is* in fact doing a lot of talking – in an earlier study we found the staff talking in 50 per cent of five second observation periods (Tizard *et al*, 1976). Yet however much the teacher talks, each child will be spoken to rather infrequently – after all, the staff-child ratio in British nursery schools and classes is at best 1:10.

Still, even this amount of talk *could* be more than many children are getting at home, and in any case the conversation at home *could* be so impoverished that even a limited input of superior quality school talk would benefit the child. In order to draw these conclusions one would have to be able to compare the language experiences of the same children at home and at school, yet up to the present this evidence has not been available.

Aim of Study

The study was devised to compare the language experiences of four year old children at home and at school. The four main areas of interest were (1) the amount of adult-child conversation in the two settings; (2) the form of the discourse — that is, such features of the conversation as who initiates and sustains it, how long conversations last, how much talk each party contributes, who asks questions. Earlier observations had suggested that there were marked differences between home and school conversations in these respects; (3) the activity context in which the conversations occurred — that is, whether adult and child were engaged in a joint activity, as distinct, for example, from a setting where the adult comments on the child's play. It seemed likely that conversations during joint activity would be longer and of greater interest to the child; (4) the adult's "curriculum", that is, what she transmits to the child and what cognitive demands she makes; (5) the role of the adult in the child's play. Only the first three sets of findings are reported below.

Method

Subjects. The subjects were 30 girls, aged between 3 years 9 months and 4 years 3 months (mean age 3 years 11 months, SD 1.8 months). Half the girls were working class, that is their fathers were manual workers and their mothers had left school at the minimum school leaving age with no educational qualifications. The other 15 girls were middle-class, that is their fathers were in professional or managerial positions, and their mothers either had had tertiary education, or had qualified for it. The other criteria were that the children should attend morning nursery school, and spend their afternoons at home with their mothers, and they should have only one or two sibs, and that the language used at home should be English. Three of the 30 girls were only children. A third of the mothers in both social classes worked part-time, in the afternoons or evenings. Of the working-class fathers, two-thirds were skilled manual workers, e.g. electricians and fitters, the rest were semi-skilled or unskilled.

The working-class children in our study could not in any reasonable sense be considered "deprived"; they lived in small, two-parent families, the majority in Council housing, and appeared to be well cared for, much loved, and plentifully supplied with toys. Since nursery schooling in Britain, although free, is not compulsory, it is possible that they came from particularly caring, or educationally orientated families. At any rate, they were probably typical of the majority of working-class children who attend half-day nursery school, and who are nevertheless seen by their teachers as in need of language enrichment.

The mean Binet IQ of the working-class girls was 106.4 (SD 13.2); of the middle-class girls 122.3 (SD 11.3). The testing was carried out by independent psychologists after the recording was completed. The children were drawn from nine different nursery schools – in each school, children from both social classes were selected. In schools where more than two children fulfilled our criteria, the study children were selected by tossing a coin. All the parents of the children who fulfilled our criteria agreed to take part in the project – that is, we were not studying a self-selected group. Two very timid children could not be persuaded to co-operate with the study, and were replaced by children from the same schools who met the criteria.

Schools. All nine schools were run by the local authorities for children aged three and four years. The children were in classes of 20–25 children, each staffed by a teacher and an assistant, usually helped by one or two students. Most of the morning was spent in free play with a wide variety of equipment. The staff role was primarily to suggest, and sometimes to demonstrate ways of using play material, and to help the children's language by informal conversation. Some of the schools also had a formal story or music sessions, for the whole class, but we excluded these sessions from our study.

Recording method. The children's mothers were asked to dress them in the mornings in a light sleeveless dress, which could be worn on its own or over a jersey or blouse. A microphone and radio transmitter was fitted into padded pockets in the dress. This equipment gave reasonably clear recordings of talk within a range of about 15 feet of the child, even in noisy nursery classes. The transmitter had a range of about 100 yards, so that the child could move freely in the home, school, garden and pavement outside. An observer followed the children around fairly closely, in order to record a detailed context of the conversations. Only adult-child, not child-child, conversations were transcribed. Further details of the equipment and methods are recorded elsewhere (Hughes *et al*, 1979).

Recording times. A pilot study in which 9 of the girls were observed for four consecutive days had shown that in the home the children's interest in the observer diminished markedly after the first day, and that there was no significant difference in the mothers' behaviour, as assessed on a number of variables, over the four day period (Hughes *et al*, 1979). In the school, however, there were systematic differences in adult-child talk over the four days, the first day being the most "deviant". We therefore decided in the main study to observe in the homes for two consecutive afternoons from about 1 p.m. – 3.30 p.m., but to use only the second day's data. In the school, we observed for three consecutive mornings from about 9 a.m. – 11.30 a.m. using only the second and third day's data. (It was necessary to collect an extra day's data at school, because the number of adult-child conversations was much smaller.) Because the pilot session had shown that large variations in the amount of adult-child talk were caused by the presence of husbands and visitors, we asked the mother to select days for recording when she did not expect anyone except herself and her children to be present. Nevertheless, visitors did occasionally call.

Intelligibility of speech

The proportion of unintelligible adult utterances averaged 1.6 per cent in the home, and 1.0 per cent in the school. For child talk, the corresponding proportions were 0.5 per cent and 1.8 per cent.

Results

Reliability

The codes described below were refined until an acceptable level of agreement between four coders on a sample of 60–80 conversations was achieved. The reliabilities of the codes (described below) were as follows; delineation of conversations, plus or minus two turns, 86 per cent; type of adult initiation, 84 per cent; type of child initiation, 94 per cent; topic of conversation, 93 per cent; nature of concurrent activity, 92 per cent; number of curiosity questions, 87 per cent; type of questions, 85 per cent; context of question, 89 per cent; type of adult response, 82 per cent; balance of conversation (number of turns in which child sustained the conversation) 84 per cent. These reliabilities are conservative, in that they refer to the presence of agreement on each individual initiation, topic, etc. not overall totals for each child.

(1) *Number of adult-child conversations.* The first task was to divide the transcript into conversations, defined as episodes of talk on the same subject, ended by a change of subject or by adult or child moving out of earshot. Table 1 shows that there was no social class difference in the hourly rate of conversations, but that many more conversations occurred at home than at school.

TABLE 1.
Hourly rate of conversations

	Working-class	Middle-class
Home	27.0	26.4
School	10.9	9.1

Location F = 119, p < 0.001. Social class NS. Interaction NS.

(2) *Length of conversation.* Table 2 shows a similar finding for length of conversation measured in "turns" of talk – there was no social class difference, but conversations at home were on average twice as long as at school, and a larger proportion of the conversations at school were very short.

(3) *Who initiated the conversations.* In all settings, children initiated a little more than half the conversations — working-class children at home, 58 per cent; at school, 51 per cent; middle-class children at home and at school, 56 per cent. These differences are not significant. The length of the conversation was not affected by who initiated it.

(4) *Why adults initiated conversation.* The reasons were coded as follows: *Control,* i.e. the child is instructed to do or not to do something, and expected to obey (this code includes threats and reprimands); *Suggestions,* concerned with play, amusement or educational matters; *Questions; Giving information and explanations,* excluding those concerned with control; *Other,* mainly praise, greetings, and "social oil". Table 3 shows that the most frequent type of adult initiation was a question. There was a significant difference in the reasons why teachers and mothers initiated conversations. Mothers of both social classes more often than teachers initiated conversations in

TABLE 2.
Length of conversations

		% of all conversations which are:			Mean episode length (turns)
		short (2–6 turns)	medium (7–21 turns)	long (22+ turns)	
Working-class at school	%	65	28	8	7.7
	N	(333)	(141)	(38)	
Middle-class at school	%	62	29	8	8.3
	N	(396)	(184)	(54)	
Working-class at home	%	43	38	18	16.5
	N	(398)	(351)	(167)	
Middle-class at home	%	42	38	20	16.1
	N	(400)	(354)	(187)	

Proportion of short, medium and long episodes: Location $X^2 = 141.p < 0.001$
Social class NS: Interaction NS.
Mean episode length: Location $F = 54.8, p < 0.001$.
Social class NS. Interaction NS.

order to inform or explain, whilst teachers more often than mothers initiated conversation with suggestions for activities and "social oil". There was also a significant interaction between social class and location, that is home-school differences were more marked for the working-class children. Their mothers more often initiated convers-

TABLE 3.
Type of adult initiation

	Control %	Suggestions %	Questions %	Information %	Other %
Working-class at school	16.5	14.4	35.4	15.2	18.5
Middle-class at school	19.0	17.5	28.7	18.3	16.4
Working-class at home	26.9	13.2	23.3	21.9	14.3
Middle-class at home	17.2	12.3	28.5	27.7	14.3

Location $X^2 = 17.6$, d.f 2, $p < 0.001$. Social class NS. Interaction $X^2 = 9.3$, d.f. 3, $p < 0.05$.

ation to control them, and less often to question them, than did middle-class mothers, whilst at school teachers questioned the working-class children more than the middle-class children.

TABLE 4
Type of child initiation

	Asks for help %	Expresses wants %	Questions %	Gives information %
Working-class at school	20.9	29.3	7.2	42.6
Middle-class at school	11.6	22.4	18.1	47.9
Working-class at home	5.3	35.8	17.5	41.4
Middle-class at home	4.8	38.4	18.0	38.8

1st and 2nd columns vs. 3rd and 4th. Location NS, Social class NS, Interaction $X^2 = 13.4$, d.f. 1, p < 0.001.

(5) *Why children initiated conversations.* The reasons were coded as, *To ask for help,* i.e. with an activity the child was unable to carry out on her own, including help in disputes with other children; *To make other kinds of demands and requests; To ask a question; To give information to the adult.* Table 4 shows that in all settings the most frequent reason for the child to initiate conversation was to tell something to the adult, and there were no social class differences at home. There was no significant home-school difference, but there was a significant interaction between social class and location. That is, there were social class differences in the reasons why children initiated conversations at school, but not at home. Working-class children more often asked for help than middle-class children —mostly in relation to disputes with other children— and they initiated fewer conversations with a question.

(6) *What the conversations were about.* The topic of the conversation was given one of the following codes: *Physical care (washing, dressing, etc); Food and meals; Friction between children; Play material or play activity; Non-play activity,* e.g. helping to cook, and also talk about people, objects or animals in the immediate environment; *TV programmes; Books and stories; The observer and/or recording equipment; The child's other life* — i.e. school at home, and home at school;

Past and future events. Table 5 shows that there was a significant home-school difference. The majority of school conversations concerned play activity, whereas at home a larger proportion were concerned with other activities, with the immediate environment, and with past or future events. There was also a significant social class difference — conversations with middle-class children more often concerned the past and the future than was the case with working-class children. In both social classes home was discussed more often at school than was school at home.

Further analysis showed that the teachers generally initiated the topic of home with the working-class children, whilst the middle-class children generally introduced this topic with the teachers. At home, the topic of school tended to be introduced by the middle-class mothers, whilst working-class mothers and children were equally likely to introduce the topic.

(7) *Length of conversation according to topic.* Table 6 shows that both at home and at school much the longest conversations concerned books which the adult was reading aloud, or had just read aloud.

(8) *Amount and kind of joint adult-child activity.* Each conversation which lasted for seven or more turns was coded as "Joint Activity" if it occurred in the course of, or interrupted, a joint adult-child activity. An activity was only coded "joint" if both adult and child were actively involved in the same activity — e.g. if both were watching and discussing TV, or tidying up or playing; if the adult was sitting talking to the child about her play this was not coded "joint activity". Table 7 shows that the amount of joint adult-child activity was much greater in homes of both social classes than at school; at both home and school there was a small non-significant tendency for the middle-class children to be more often engaged in joint activity with adults. The somewhat surprising finding that there were more stories in the working-class homes than the middle-class homes was because the peak story time in the middle-class homes was in the evening. The larger amount of "joint" TV watching in the middle-class homes was not because the TV was switched on for longer periods than in the working-class homes, but because middle-class mothers more often sat and watched it with their children. Similarly, middle-class mothers more often sat down to a meal with their children, whilst working-class children more

TABLE 5.
Topic of conversation

	(1) Physical care + food	(2) Disputes between children	(3) Play	(4) Non- play activity + TV	(5) Books	(6) Observer + equipment	(7) Child's other life	(8) Past and future
	%	%	%	%	%	%	%	%
Working-class school	17 N (87)	4 (23)	55 (283)	16 (84)	1 (6)	0 (1)	5 (25)	1 (3)
Middle-class school	18 N (116)	1 (8)	50 (318)	19 (118)	2 (12)	0 (1)	8 (48)	2 (13)
Working-class home	22 N (198)	1 (8)	34 (311)	30 (271)	1 (11)	3 (24)	3 (25)	7 (68)
Middle-class home	23 N (212)	1 (9)	32 (305)	28 (260)	1 (10)	3 (25)	3 (32)	9 (88)

Distribution of columns 1; 3; 4; 7 plus 8.
Location $X^2 = 116$, d.f.3, $p < 0.001$.
Class $X^2 = 10.0$, d.f.3, $p < 0.05$. Interaction NS.

TABLE 6

Length of conversation according to topic (Data in body of Table refer to 'Mean turns')

	physical care + food	Disputes between children	Play	Non-play activity + TV	Books	Observer + equipment	Child's other life	Past + future
Working-class school	6.3	4.2	8.8	5.4	35.2	3.0	11.3	8.3
Middle-class school	5.6	7.1	9.9	5.1	27.2	7.0	11.3	14.5
Working-class home	10.3	5.3	21.8	10.3	54.1	11.0	12.6	18.7
Middle-class home	12.7	7.9	24.0	9.9	32.4	5.6	12.5	14.6

(Insufficient numbers in some cells for analysis.)

TABLE 7.
Amount and type of joint activity

	Joint play	Joint non-play activity	Joint stories	Joint TV watching	Joint meals	Joint physical care	All joint activity
		Mean hourly rate, measured in "turns" of conversation					
Working-class at school	11.9	1.4	3.7	0	0	3.1	20.2
Middle-class at school	25.9	1.8	6.3	0	0	1.1	34.9
Working-class at home	90.1	19.7	12.6	1.9	22.1	6.0	152.3
Middle-class at home	100.9	22.5	7.7	8.0	45.3	4.2	188.5

Hourly rate of Joint Activity: Location $F = 35.6 < 0.001$.
Social class NS Interaction NS.

TABLE 8
Length of conversation and type of activity

	Joint play	Joint non-play activity	Joint stories	Joint TV watching	Joint meals	Joint physical care	No. joint activity
			Mean number of turns per conversation				
Working-class school	22	15	31	0	0	17	15
Middle-class school	27	17	31	0	0	16	13
Working-class home	57	51	49	18	24	25	19
Middle-class home	51	49	52	25	20	16	19

(Conversations of 7 or less turns are excluded: some cells too small for analysis.)

often ate on their own or wandered around with a sandwich.

(9) *Length of conversation and type of activity.* Table 8 shows that both at school and home conversations tended to be longer when adult and child were engaged on a joint activity, especially when they were discussing books or playing together.

(10) *Number and type of questions.* Table 9 shows that the children asked very few questions at school and very many at home, and that there was no significant social class difference. (Certain categories of question, e.g. requests, offers, repetitions of other's questions were not coded as questions.) The questions were coded as either "specific", i.e. about a specific object, person, or event (e.g. What colour is that?) or "non-specific", i.e. questions which went beyond a specific object or event, by asking for an explanation, prediction or generalisation (e.g. Why are you doing that? Do frogs live in the sea?)

TABLE 9
Hourly rate of questions

	Working-class N	Middle-class N
School	1.4	3.7
Home	24.0	29.0

Location F = 77.4, p < 0.001, Social class NS. Interaction NS.

Table 10 shows that both at home and school middle-class children asked a higher proportion of "non-specific" (i.e. why and how questions) than working-class children, and children of both social classes asked a higher proportion of "non-specific" questions at home than at school.

(11) *Context of questions.* The questions were categorised according to whether they occurred in the context of control (e.g. "Put that down" — "Why?") or because the answer was needed to carry out an ongoing activity (e.g. "Where are the scissors?") or were "non-control" curiosity questions (e.g. "Is the baby asleep?" not asked in either of these contexts). Table 11 shows that a smaller proportion of questions at school were "non-control" curiosity questions, and this

TABLE 10
Type of question

	Specific questions		Non-specific questions	
	Total	%	Total	%
Working-class at school	62	85	11	15
Middle-class at school	167	78	46	22
Working-class at home	645	78	178	22
Middle-class at home	701	69	309	31

(Insufficient non-specific questions at school for analysis)

ʷas particularly true of the working-class children, who also asked
few   ᵃf these questions at home than did middle-class children.

TABLE 11.
Context of questions

	A Questions in control situations		B Questions needed for activity		C Curiosity questions	
	Total	%	Total	%	Total	%
Working-class at school	5	7	50	70	17	24
Middle-class at school	4	2	76	36	131	62
Working-class at home	107	13	271	34	426	53
Middle-class at home	76	8	198	20	716	72

(Insufficient A & C questions at school for analysis. The number of questions in this
table is slightly less than in Table 10, because of difficulty in coding some questions for
context.)

(12) *Number of questions and topic of conversation.* In all settings,
the mean number of questions per conversation was highest in conversations about books, and then in conversations about past and future
events.

(13) *Adult response to questions.* The way in which the adults
responded to the children's questions is shown in Table 12. Most questions were answered, although only a small minority received an "elaborate" answer — arbitrarily defined as an answer containing more than
one main verb. The proportion of "elaborate" answers was higher at
school than at home — perhaps because many more questions were

TABLE 12.
Adults' responses to questions

	N	Child answers own + question	Adult mis-hears mis-under-stands	Turns question round	Asks for clari-fication	Gives adequate answer	Gives elaborate answer	No answer
		%	%	%	%	%	%	%
Working-class school	71	2.8	9.9	5.6	1.4	46.5	22.5	11.3
Middle-class school	209	1.9	5.3	5.3	1.9	44.4	27.3	13.9
Working-class home	799	4.4	6.8	1.8	1.9	58.2	13.3	13.6
Middle-class home	976	3.2	4.8	2.2	2.4	55.9	21.5	10.0

(Some cells too small to permit analysis.)

asked at home — and both at home and at school middle-class children were more often given "elaborate" answers.

(14) *Amount of talk contributed by adult and child.* Table 13 shows that whilst teachers spoke significantly longer per turn of talk than mothers, the children's turns were significantly shorter at school than at home. There were no social class differences in the length of adult turns, but there was a tendency for working-class children to use shorter turns at school than at home.

TABLE 13.
Length of adult and child turns

	Adult	Child
	Mean number of words per turn	
Working-class at school	14.0	4.8
Middle-class at school	14.5	5.4
Working-class at home	6.5	5.8
Middle-class at home	8.6	5.8

Based on 11 randomly chosen conversations per child per setting.
Mean adult words per hour: Location $F = 37.5$, $p < 0.001$.
Social Class N.S. Interaction: N.S. Mean child words per turn
Location $F = 4.8$, $p < 0.05$, Social class: N.S. Interaction N.S.
Proportion of adult to child talk: Location $F = 50.8$, $p < 0.001$.
Social class N.S. Interaction $F = 3.97$, $p < 0.06$.

(15) *Who sustains the conversation?* Each turn in a conversation was coded according to whether it initiated or sustained the conversation, or was only a reply or an acknowledgement. All questions, commands and demands sustain a conversation, because they oblige a response; new comments made as well as, or instead of, a response also sustain a conversation. Table 14 shows that at home mothers and children made a nearly equal contribution to sustaining the conversation, but that at school the conversations tended to be sustained by the teacher. This was because the typical school conversation tended to take the form of a series of questions from the staff and answers from the child.

There was a tendency, which nearly approached significance, for working-class children to sustain conversation more often than middle-class children at home, but less often at school. Table 14 also

TABLE 14.
Sustaining the conversation

		% of conversation sustained by child N = 165	Mean % child does not respond
Working-class at school		15	15.6
	N	(24)	
Middle-class at school		23	11.4
	N	(38)	
Working-class at home		48	6.6
	N	(79)	
Middle-class at home		45	7.1
	N	(74)	

Based on 11 randomly chosen conversations per child per setting.
Child sustains, Location X^2 = 58.5, d.f. 1, p < 0.001.
Social class N.S. Interaction X^2 = 3.61, d.f. 1. p < 0.01.
Child doesn't answer, Location F = 21.1 p < 0.001, Social class N.S.
Interaction N.S.

shows that children were significantly more likely not to answer the adult at school than at home.

(16) *Relationship between child's conversation at home and at school.* Correlations between scores on all the variables considered at home and at school were low and not significant — that is, there was no tendency for a child who talked a lot or asked a lot of questions or who tended to initiate conversation at home to do so at school.

(17) *Relationship between child's IQ and other measures.* There was a tendency for the working-class children with higher IQs to talk more at school (r= +0.53, p < 0.04) and ask more questions at school (r = +0.56, p < 0.03) than those of lower IQ. There was also a tendency for the working-class children with higher IQs to ask a greater proportion of "Non-control" questions at home (i.e. not in the context of control or of carrying out an activity) (r = +0.6, p < 0.05). In the case of the middle-class children all these correlations were very small and in the opposite direction. There was a tendency for the middle-class children of higher IQ to initiate fewer conversations with their mothers with an appeal or a demand than did those of lower IQ (r = −0.54, p < 0.04). Correlations between all the other variables and IQ were very low, and

often in the opposite direction in the two social classes. For this reason an analysis of co-variance including IQ was not considered appropriate.

Discussion

The principal aim of this study was to compare the language experiences of young children at home and at nursery school, in an attempt to understand the educational role of mothers and teachers. There are, of course, many ways in which conversations can be evaluated; in this paper we have largely focussed on the overall structure of the discourse, in our next paper we shall consider the content of what is said.

The most striking finding in the present analysis was that, for the majority of variables considered, home school differences were very large and social class differences at home very small or absent. This was true with respect to the hourly rate of conversations, the length of conversations, the hourly rate of questions, the relative amount of talk contributed to the conversation by the adult and child, the extent to which the adult rather than the child kept the conversation going, and the frequency with which the child answered the adult. That is, at home conversations were more frequent, longer, and more equally balanced between adult and child; further, children of both social classes asked questions at home much more frequently than at school, and answered adults more often.

It is, of course, very understandable that a teacher with a whole class to look after should hold fewer and briefer conversations with a child than its mother. But equally, it is important to note that the mother has an educational advantage in this respect. In the course of a long conversation a theme can be discussed from a number of different standpoints, other areas of the child's experience can be related, misunderstandings can emerge and be clarified.

This point can be illustrated by extracts from two conversations, the only instances in the study of the same subject being discussed by a child at home and at school, Ann's mother was expecting twins. In the morning the subject was touched on by Ann's teacher in a 5-turn conversation, at home in the afternoon Ann did a drawing of the expected babies during a 60-turn conversation, an extract of which is printed below.

Conversations I and II

Talking about the expected twins (middle-class child)

HOME		SCHOOL
Ann:	Come and look at their little bit of hair.	*T:* What are you going to call your babies?
M:	Love, I'm just looking for Ben's shorts, I don't know what he's done with them.	Hm?
		What are you going to call your twins? Ann?
Ann:	Hum, look at his . . . Mum look at his little sh . . . look at his little h . . . Mummy, he's got a little bit hair, so come and have a look.	*Ann:* Emily and Katy.
M:	Blue hair (laughs)	*T:* Emily. . .?
Anne:	What's wrong with blue hair?	*Ann:* And Katy.
M:	Well I don't know, it can be fair hair, or brown hair, or red hair.	*T:* Katy!
Ann:	Don't have red hair. (indignant).	Supposing they're boys? You can't call twins that if they're boys can you?
M:	Some people do. Know that boy in the park yesterday?	(laughs)
Ann:	Yea.	(Ann laughs and goes off)
M:	With a kite.	
Ann:	Yea, Mummy.	
M:	He had what you call red hair, auburn.	
	You know Daddy?	
Ann:	Mm.	
M:	He used to have red hair, before it went grey.	

The second example is of two conversations which followed an incident in the sandpit at school when the wind had blown the buckets about.

Conversations III and IV

A windy day (working-class child)

HOME		SCHOOL	
M:	Was the wind blowing the sand at your nursery?	*Jean:*	I'm telling Mummy that the buckets rolled away.
Jean:	Yea.	*M:*	Pardon?
M:	Hm. The sand is all dry now and when it's windy . . .	*Jean:*	I'm telling Mummy that the buckets rolled away, when we were not looking.
Jean:	And it went right in my eyes, and Mummy I want to tell you something. And it's funny, um, the buckets rolled away and. . . and, we wasn't looking there . . . and we said . . . and we weren't able to catch the buckets.	*T:*	Are you?
		Jean:	Yea.
		T:	That's nice.
		Jean:	A-and the sand went a-all in my eyes.
M:	Weren't you?	*T:*	In your eyes? Were they sore?
Jean:	No.		Are they still sore now? Oh, you poor old thing. Do you think if you had a piece of apple, it would make them feel better?
M:	And what was making the buckets run away? Because they haven't got legs, have they?		
Jean:	No.	*Jean:*	It was in there.
M:	Then what was making them run away?	*T:*	O'kay, well let's wash it out.
Jean:	Rolling.		(T and Jean go to bathroom)
M:	They were rolling?		

Jean:	Yea. Yea. They were rolling . . . see, they were standing up, and we was not looking, 'cos, we was making sand castles.
M:	Mm.
Jean:	And then we was not looking.
M:	Mm.
Jean:	And then it tumbled over, the buckets, and then it went roll, roll, roll. 'Cos the wind blow huff.
M:	Oh gosh. Very strong the wind, isn't it?
Jean:	Yea.

It is apparent from reading these extracts that a much deeper exchange of meaning was occurring at home than at school. At home, there is a note of urgency, even of excitement in the children's communications; Ann's mother supplies general knowledge, and connects up areas of the child's experience; she and Ann feel free to criticise and contradict each other. Jean's mother is intent on encouraging her to recall and understand an event in detail. In contrast, both teachers fail to retain the child's interest, or in Jean's case, misinterpret the nature of her concern.

The potential educational advantage of the home is also evident when one considers the child's contribution to the conversation at school and at home, in terms of sustaining the conversation and asking questions. At school, the teacher tends to dominate the conversation (as in the examples above). At home, the child's contribution, in the form of sustaining comments, and in particular of questions, is much greater.

Surprisingly, perhaps, in view of the child-centred free play orientation of the nursery school, the pedagogical approach revealed by this analysis is right in the main stream of traditional education — the teacher's exchange with each child is brief, and during it she dominates, and questions; the child's role is to answer.

Clearly, in some situations this pedagogical approach is appropriate, and it may be argued that the adult, because of her greater knowledge and experience *should* direct and sustain the conversation and do most of the talking. But exchanges of this kind have serious drawbacks, if they are seen as a major educational medium for young children.

Firstly, the child gets relatively little practice in expressing herself — compare the amount and the vividness of the child's talk at home and at school in the examples above. Secondly, if we view the young child's intellectual development as in large part her own construction, in which she learns through her own encounters with the social and material world, then her questions can be seen to play a key role in her development. This is because her questions serve to focus adult talk on what is of real concern to the child, and because they reveal her uncertainties, confusions, and misunderstandings, which the adult can try to clarify.

An extract from such a conversation in a working-class home is quoted below.

Conversation V
Talk about a speech therapist

HOME	CONTEXT
M: Oh, Joan. You've got to go and see another lady on Tuesday	Joan, Mother, and younger brother Sean sitting in living room, eating chocolate.
Joan: What lady?	
M: Another lady wants to hear you.	Joan has a speech difficulty.
Joan: What lady?	
M: The lady at the clinic wants to hear you speaking on Tuesday.	M refers to the speech therapist.

Joan:	. . . where . . . goes?	Joan asks if it's the place where a friend goes.
M:	No, where you got your ears tested.	She had her ears tested at the clinic earlier.
	She's going to learn you how to say your words properly.	Joan is going to have a few sessions with the therapists.
	She's going to say them, and you've got to say them after her.	
Joan:	I don't know all the words.	
M:	Yeah. But she's going to learn you.	
	She's going to teach them to you.	
Joan:	What's her name?	Joan refers to the speech therapist.
M:	Em . . . Miss Jenkins.	
Joan:	And . . . that's where I got my ears tested?	
M:	Where you got your ears tested then.	
Joan:	That's where I'm going.	
M:	Mm-m.	
Joan:	Sean mus'nt make a noise.	Presumably Sean was told to be quiet during the hearing test last time.
M:	That was when you were getting your ears tested, he musn't make a noise.	
Joan:	No.	*M*. No reply.

The study yielded some social class differences which obtained both at home and school. Middle-class children more often discussed other than "here-and-now" topics, more often engaged in joint activity with adults, asked more "how" and "why" questions, and more often asked "non-control" curiosity questions, as opposed to questions needed in order to carry out an activity, or questions arising in relation to control. There was no relationship between IQ and the first two of these differences. Within the working-class group there was some tendency for the girls with higher IQ to ask more "non-control" curiosity questions at home.

These social class differences were relatively small compared to the home-school differences — e.g. although middle-class children asked over one and a half times as many "why" and "how" questions at home as working-class children, working-class children asked sixteen times as many such questions at home as they did at school.

There were, in addition, some interactions between social class and setting, that is, variables on which social class differences were found at school but not at home. At school, working-class children more often than middle-class children approached the teacher for help in disputes, and less often to ask questions, or give information. Working-class children also tended to make a smaller contribution to teacher-child conversations than middle-class children — to speak more briefly, and less often keep the conversation going — although at home there were no social class differences in these respects. These findings accord with the observers' impressions that the working-class children appeared "less confident" at school than the middle-class children. There was also evidence of a greater contrast between teacher and mother behaviour for working-class than middle-class children with respect to the frequency of control, and of adult's questions.

It would be premature to discuss the general implications of the study, without an analysis of what was being discussed. The finding that both at school and at home the longest conversations tended to occur in the context of story-reading and joint adult-child play, and that the context which provoked most questions from the children was story-telling, is of immediate relevance to teachers. Our findings do, in addition, suggest that professionals should be very cautious in drawing inferences about a child's language competence from his speech performance outside his home setting. We found no consistent relationship between the way the children talked at home and at school, with respect, e.g. to the number of questions asked or the amount of talk. Further, the working-class children in particular were relatively muted, even in the informal free play regimen of the nursery school. A professional's conclusion that the children's language was deficient, on the basis of their speech in this setting, might therefore have been mistaken.

Our findings also suggest that professionals' advice to mothers on how to talk to their children may often be wide of the mark. The mothers in our study played much more with their children, talked to them much more, answered many more questions than did the teachers. It is, of course, true that all the families in our study were small, two-parent families, who had chosen to send their children to nursery school, and that very different results might have obtained in large families. But it is for families such as these in our study that teachers saw the main gain of nursery education as "extending language".

It is also true that the characteristics of the conversations may well have been affected by the presence of an observer. Yet it is not easy to see how this factor could have produced the pattern of results which we found. It seems more likely that the results reflect systematic differences in the social relationships between children and the adults looking after them. Readiness to question, to comment on the other's remarks, to contribute one's own reflexions and experiences, depends on the relative status of the participants in the conversation and the degree of intimacy between them. This is as true at a post-graduate seminar as at nursery school. So long as the teacher is a relatively remote stranger, operating in an environment very different from the child's home, the child will not talk freely with her, and she is likely to form a false impression of the child. A better understanding of the learning environment at home would seem a prerequisite to any attempt to help or advise parents.

Acknowledgements

We would like to acknowledge the co-operation of the teachers, parents and children in the study, and the statistical help of Ian Plewis and Charles Owen.

References

Bullock Report (1975) *A Language for Life,* D.E.S., H.M.S.O.
Hughes, M., Tizard, B., Carmichael, H. and Pinkerton, G. (1979) Recording children's conversations at home and at school: a technique and some methodological considerations, *Journal of Child Psychol. Psychiat.* Vol. 20, pp. 225–32.

Tizard, B. (1975) *Early Childhood Education*, A Review and Discussion of current research in Britain, N.F.E.R., Slough.

Tizard, B. Philps, J. and Plewis, I. (1976) Staff behaviour in Pre-school centres, *J. Child Psychol. Psychiat*, **17**, 21–33.

Tizard, B. (1977) No Common Ground, *Times Education Supplement*, **15**.

Wells, G. (1975) *Language Development in Pre-school Children*, Unpublished Report, University of Bristol.

Wootton, A. (1974) Talk in the homes of young children, *Sociology*, **8**, 277.

CHAPTER 4

Syndrome Delineation in Communication Disorders

J. A. M. MARTIN

Nuffield Hearing and Speech Centre
Royal National Throat, Nose and Ear Hospital, London.

Language disorder in the child is an absorbing subject which touches on many clinical disciplines, yet it has been curiously neglected medically. There is an extensive and ever expanding literature on the subject of child language, mostly from the research disciplines centred on cognitive psychology and linguistic science, see for example Bloom (1970), Brown (1973), Bruner (1975), Fourcin (1978), Whitaker (1976).

It might seem reasonable to assume that the theoretical problems which exist between the meaning of what is said or written and the form and structure of the utterance encapsulating that meaning, are well understood. This is not so. Despite the antiquity of the origins of interest in words, in grammar, logic and rhetoric, linguistics as a science is a surprisingly new discipline. Its concepts, and even its vocabulary change rapidly and what was recently accorded the authority of formal doctrine may quite soon be held suspect or become untenable. It would be unwise therefore to venture into any theoretical discussion here about the nature of language disorder in the child. Instead, patterns of language disability will be discussed from a clinical viewpoint based on what one may observe and assess, relying on a detailed, developmental approach.

Nature of Material

The clinical material consists of a personal series of 315 children seen for the first time since the beginning of January 1975 up to the middle of 1977. The children are unselected, with the exception that those in whom the data were inadequate for completion of the proforma used in the analysis, were excluded. They form part of a larger series totalling 830 going back to January 1970. At that time the children with hearing loss were not recorded in such detail, interest (for research purposes) centering on the child who had some form of spoken language deficit without deafness. With increasing experience it has become abundantly clear that childhood deafness is not a separate clinical entity, but instead forms one particular stratum of language disorder in children. It was thought appropriate to present a more limited series numerically, but one which is full inclusive for range and type of disability, and in which the data are strictly comparable for all the children seen.

Collection of Data and Analysis of Results

The information contained in the case notes and in a standard questionnaire, sent to all parents before they attend the Nuffield Hearing and Speech Centre for the first time, was transcribed and recoded on to a proforma containing just under 80 data points. These include the usual identification material, age, sex, family history of the disability, intrauterine, birth and postnatal details and ten major sections, each one of which is made up of a number of specific items.

(1) *Speech*. The quality of the voice, the range of tonal variation, its rhythm and fluency; and the accuracy of articulation for the consonants and vowels of spoken English, due consideration being given to the overall level of linguistic development of the child.

(2) *Verbal Expression*. The age at which single words were first used purposefully, the rate of vocabulary development, the appearance of word joining. In assessment, the typical length of the utterance, and the accuracy, range and complexity of the syntax being used.

(3) *Hearing*. This is measured to the nearest 5 dB wherever possible. Children in whom it is not possible to obtain accurate thresholds

either in free field or by standard pure tone audiometry have their hearing estimated by a simple acoustic reflex method or failing this by electrocochleography and/or brain-stem evoked response audiometry.

4. *Verbal Comprehension.* It is essential both in the course of obtaining the history from the parents, and in the process of clinical assessment, to make sure that the child is responding to the spoken word and not to the prevailing situation, or by habit and long-standing association, or through the mediation of various signs and gestures made by hand or other parts of the body. Information is required on the length and complexity of the utterance spoken to the child, and it is essential to have clear evidence of his ability to understand and carry out what has been said to him.

5. *General motor development and function.* This includes information on the major milestones of motor development, the quality of the posture, gait and manipulation, the coordination and control of movement as a whole, and the presence of specific patterns of deranged motor function.

6. *Motor function of the speech apparatus.* The changing patterns of facial expression, the shape and tone of the lips, the tongue and the movements of the soft palate all give information on the quality of motor control in the component parts of the speech apparatus. The tongue in particular requires careful observation both at rest and when the child is being asked to carry out various movements. Impaired function may be revealed by the presence of involuntary activity and imprecision, either for single movements or for repetitive groups of movements.

7. *Intelligence.* It is important to ensure that those carrying out these assessments are confident in their ability to communicate with children having various types of language deficit. Similarly, test scales must be chosen carefully to avoid any adverse loading of the overall result by specifically linguistic items.

8. *Play.* The child's understanding of the significance of a variety of items, graded in complexity from commonly occurring household objects through a doll's tea set to miniature doll's house furniture and mannikins, is assessed during the course of the clinic visit. It derives from the work of Sheridan (1977) and provides so much useful information that it has been for some years a standard clinical procedure.

9. *Maturity and behaviour.* This may be assessed in part on a standardised scale such as the Vineland; much may be gained from careful history-taking and observation though a child may behave very differently in the confines of a clinic room however much the layout and atmosphere are adapted to suit the child. Particular points to be assessed are the way in which the child relates to the various adults in the room once he has been given the opportunity to settle down in unfamiliar surroundings; his interest in, and ability to cooperate and to participate in the activities and play materials made available; and his desire to communicate with those around him however limited his actual verbal resources may be.

10. *Family background.* In order to avoid any unduly impressionistic approach this is confined to specific points such as the availability of both parents, the degree of accord between them, their attitude to the child and to his handicap and the stability of care which they can provide.

It is not easy to gain more than a very approximate idea of these last two factors until the family, and the clinicians, therapists and teachers have known each other for some time; the importance of information from those who can visit the home such as health visitors and social workers cannot be overstressed. It is essential to avoid any off-the-cuff scoring of the child, and of his parents' attitudes and abilities at child-rearing. One sees a surprising number of superficial judgements made on the basis of a brief, bewildering visit to hospital. We are in need of a more objective procedure which will provide information on the degree of stimulation in the home, the quality of interpersonal communication, or the parents' intuitive skills or deficits as language modellers when they are denied the normal processes of feedback from their child.

Scaling

Each feature within these ten major components of the profile is scored on a three point scale. In those instances where a great deal of information is available for a single entry point, as for instance the non-verbal performance IQ of the WISC (Wechsler, 1949) or Bayley, (1935) or Snijders, J. Th. & Snijders-Oomen, N., (1959) scales, or the verbal comprehension measured on the Reynell Developmental scale (Reynell, 1969) or the syntactical quality of expressive language by Crystal's procedure (Crystal, Fletcher & Garman, 1976), then a ten point scale is used. From these entries for individual features an overall average is obtained for each of the ten major components outlined above. Reference to Table 1 shows the numerical basis for the scaling of disability. The lowest line shows the level of ability in relation to the chronological age, expressed as a percentage.

TABLE 1

DEFINITION OF LEVEL OF ABILITY EXPRESSED
AS FUNCTION OF CHRONOLOGICAL AGE

NORMAL (0) ABILITY	MODERATE (1) IMPAIRMENT	SEVERE (2) IMPAIRMENT
0 1 2 3	4 5 6 7	8 9
100 90	80 70	60 50

This is valid for several of the components, but it is not appropriate for the threshold of hearing. The scale above this converts the ability to a decimal scale, and also represents the actual level of hearing loss in decibels, averaged out for the three frequencies — 250 Hz, 1 kHz and 4 kHz. Exactly where the limits should be set when transforming all this into a more clinically appropriate three point scale is open to debate. It is suggested that "Normal" (0) includes an ability of 85 per cent of

normal, that "Moderate impairment" (1) ranges from 80 per cent
down to 65 per cent and that "Severe impairment" (2) is 60 per cent or
less. If a child of 4.0 years is talking like a child of 3.0 years he is functioning at a level corresponding to 75 per cent of normal average
development, and this is a moderate but significant degree of disability. If a 30 month old child understands what is said to her no better
than one aged 12—15 months she is functioning at a level of verbal
comprehension which is equivalent to 50 per cent of average normal
and has a severe disability. It is doubtful that any more precise categorisation is helpful for clinical purposes.

Clinical Relationships Observed between Components

The age distribution of the 315 children included in the series is
shown in Fig. 1.

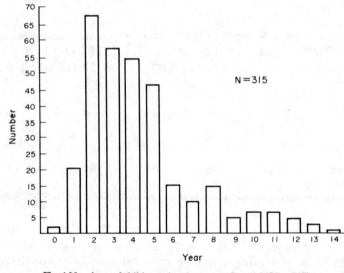

Fig. 1 Numbers of children, showing age at first visit (N = 315)

The greatest number attended for the first time when they were two
years old, and the numbers remain high until after the fifth birthday is
reached, following when there is a marked decrease.

Hearing and verbal expression.

The interrelationship between hearing and spoken language is shown in Table 2. In this group of children all those who have any degree of impairment of non-verbal comprehension — a term which will be considered in more detail below — have been excluded, so that we are looking at children who show no form of cognitive deficit other than language.

TABLE 2

THE RELATIONSHIP OF HEARING LOSS TO VERBAL COMPREHENSION & EXPRESSION

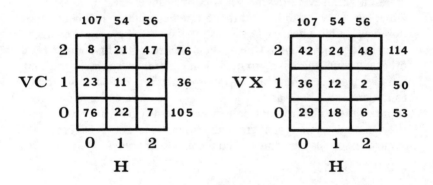

	107	54	56	
VC 2	8	21	47	76
VC 1	23	11	2	36
VC 0	76	22	7	105
	0	1	2	
		H		

	107	54	56	
VX 2	42	24	48	114
VX 1	36	12	2	50
VX 0	29	18	6	53
	0	1	2	
		H		

All children with any impairment of non-verbal comprehension excluded   N=217

It may be seen that half the children have a hearing loss, slightly more than one third of the series as a whole. A puzzling feature concerning the distribution of the degree of hearing loss is that children with a severe or profound deafness are as numerous as those in whom the loss is only moderately severe. It is reasonable to expect that the more severe the degree of hearing loss the greater the impairment of expressive ability, and this is confirmed in the 48 children in whom there is severe impairment both of hearing and verbal expression. What is surprising however is that of the 107 children with normal or near normal hearing, 78 had some degree of impairment of expressive language, and in over half of them this was severe. It will be recalled that none of these children had any significant degree of intellectual handicap.

Hearing and verbal comprehension

When one turns to the relationship between hearing and the child's ability to understand what is said to him, it may be seen (Table 2) that the total for severe impairment of both components is virtually the same as for verbal expression. One remarkable finding is that seven children with severe deafness had normal understanding for spoken language. It needs to be said that a number of these had been diagnosed as having a hearing loss and started on the appropriate management before they attended the Nuffield Centre for the first time. At the other extreme, there is a group of eight children in whom hearing and intelligence was normal but who showed a severe deficit in the ability to understand what was said to them. In the more extreme instance, some of these children not only cannot identify particular words but they cannot even make gross discriminations between commonly occurring sounds going on around them in their homes.

Non-verbal comprehension in relation to language

Non-verbal comprehension is a term used here to represent the child's overall level of cognitive behaviour and function after the exclusion of verbal processing skills. Intelligence as measured by the psychologist using the performance items of one or more of the standard scales, is not adequate by itself as a measure of non-verbal cognitive functioning. In some language disordered children there is evidence of some basic cognitive deficit affecting the ability to perceive details of the environment, their significance and interrelationships. This is revealed by an impaired ability to grasp the symbolic meaning encapsulated in such play materials as dolls, miniature tea-sets, dolls-house furniture; it is demonstrated by the way in which these objects are handled to recreate and organise them into a personal replica of the world around. The parents' description and the child's play need to be studied carefully. Because a child pushes a toy car around endlessly, or lines up his collection of them in a long column does not mean that he has understood the true nature of the object he is manipulating. In other children one gains the impression that the quality of the child's play is poor because of the lack on the part of his parents to provide a suitably stimulating environment. It may be for some parents that domestic circumstances simply do not permit them to provide this, and one must be cautious of any judgemental interpretation of such data until a more detailed picture of the home background is available. Table 3 shows the relationship between non-verbal cognitive ability and verbal comprehension and expression.

TABLE 3

THE RELATIONSHIP OF NON-VERBAL COMPREHENSION
TO VERBAL COMPREHENSION & EXPRESSION

VC

	107	37	31	
2	8	14	30	52
1	23	22	1	46
0	76	1		77
	0	1	2	

NVC

VX

	107	37	31	
2	42	30	31	103
1	36	7		43
0	29			29
	0	1	2	

NVC

All children with hearing loss excluded
N=175

One would predict that there is some correlation between the degree of overall retardation and the extent of impairment of language function, but the findings in practice are more complex. Out of 37 children in whom there was only moderate impairment of non-verbal cognitive function, 30 had a severe deficit of spoken language quite apart from articulatory problems. The results for verbal comprehension are rather better, but there remain 14 out of the same 37 children with severely defective verbal comprehension. It should be noted that from this group, totalling 175 children, all those with any significant degree of hearing loss have been excluded.

The relation between verbal expression and comprehension

The relationship between the two major components of language usage, the ability to understand what is said, and to express oneself in words, is shown for two differing populations in Table 4.

TABLE 4

THE RELATIONSHIP OF VERBAL COMPREHENSION & VERBAL EXPRESSION

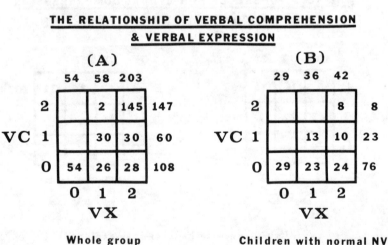

(A)

	54	58	203	
VC 2		2	145	147
VC 1		30	30	60
VC 0	54	26	28	108
	0	1	2	

VX

Whole group

N=315

(B)

	29	36	42	
VC 2			8	8
VC 1		13	10	23
VC 0	29	23	24	76
	0	1	2	

VX

Children with normal NVC and normal hearing only

N=107

Group A is the whole series, and is to be compared with Group B which includes only those children (totalling 107) with normal hearing and non-verbal comprehension. In the full series the very large number of children with severe impairment both of comprehension and expression is particularly noticeable, forming 46 per cent of the total. The difference between the two groups indicates that the majority of these children suffered either from severe hearing loss, or from severe retardation, or in some unfortunate children from both these handicaps in combination.

Sex ratios

For the series as a whole the ratio of boys to girls is 2.1 : 1 (Table 5).

TABLE 5

SEX RATIO FOR SPECIFIED GROUPS

	BOYS	GIRLS	RATIO	TOTAL
Normal hearing & NVC	81	26	3·1	107
All with hearing loss	85	55	1·5	140
All with impaired NVC	46	22	2·1	68
Whole group	212	103	2·1	315

If the children with hearing loss and impaired non-verbal comprehension are excluded, the ratio of boys to girls rises to 3.1 : 1. It is lowest for the children with hearing loss, though there is still a preponderance of boys, and the group in whom hearing loss has been excluded but who show some degree of impairment of intelligence reflect the ratio of the overall series.

Formulation of Handicap

It is essential to arrive at a single formulation of the child's level of abilities expressed in relation to normal development. This does not mean of course that the problems of the children we are considering are necessarily developmental. On the contrary, there are disorders which are not themselves developmental such as certain patterns of motor disability, deafness, and various forms of perceptual dysfunction other than hearing loss. These disorders will affect the ordered acquisition of particular skills and abilities. It is convenient and meaningful to chart the level of attainment of the child and his rate of progress in developmental terms, but it is important to retain the distinction between cause and effect.

The first approach to an understanding of the nature and extent of the child's language disorder is to assess his verbal expression (VX), verbal comprehension (VC) and non-verbal comprehension (NVC) in relation to his chronological age (CA). These four terms are arranged in the order

$$CA : NVC : VC : VX$$

and the relationship between each term, indicated by the colon, is determined on the basis of the clinical findings. Using the three gradings of "Normal" (O), "Moderately impaired" (1), or "Severely impaired" (2), these relations are indicated by conventional symbols

$=$ is equal to;

$\geq$ is equal to, or greater than, implying an element of uncertainty which can be resolved subsequently;

$>$ is greater than, the inequality being a difference of one grade;

$>>$ is much greater than, the inequality being a difference of two grades.

The formulation, despite its initial strangeness, is not so complicated as it appears and proves in practice to be an economical and meaningful way of summarising the essential characteristics of the child's relevant abilities.

The sequential arrangement of the terms, and the possible relationships which can exist between them carry certain important implications. To consider first VX, this cannot be better than VC. There are in fact occasions when it appears that this rule is broken, but they are invariably artefacts, usually resulting from the style of training the child has received. A deaf child or a mentally retarded child can be taught to utter certain verbal formulas which convey a spurious impression of ability well above the child's ability to understand what such utterances actually mean. This is of course a consequence of the undue emphasis on making a child talk, an approach by no means confined to parents. Turning to VC, this normally cannot be better than NVC. The corollary is that if verbal comprehension is found to be normal, one need have no anxiety about a significant degree of mental retardation being present. In any case of doubt, it is essential to refer the child to a psychological colleague who is thoroughly conversant with the problems of assessing non-verbal performance in the presence of hearing loss or other forms of impaired language function.

The way in which the equations are formulated and the implications they carry for further assessment or for management is best shown by some examples.

(1) $CA = VC > VX$

Starting with the final term, the child's ability to talk is moderately impaired but his ability to understand what is said to him is age appropriate. The question remains open about the cause of impaired VX. The child's difficulty may be due to inability to use the full range of linguistic structures appropriate to his age; or the neuromotor control of the speech apparatus may be impaired so that he is simply not able to produce the sounds, or the sounds in rapid sequence, or can only produce one or two words with great difficulty when he should be speaking in sentences several words long; or the two deficits may, and frequently do, occur together.

(2) $CA = NVC >> VC = VX$

Verbal expression is severely impaired, but so also is the child's ability to understand what is said to him. Whenever VC is impaired the possibility of mental retardation must be considered. In this child NVC is normal. The other possibility is that there is a hearing loss, and it is obligatory to arrive at a decision on the auditory threshold. If this also is within normal limits, one may conclude that the child has some form of receptive language disorder. In view of the rarity of this type of condition, and the many erroneous results of hearing tests, further competent audiological investigation is inevitably required.

(3)   CA > NVC = VC ⩾ VX

Both verbal expression and comprehension are moderately impaired, expressive ability being probably rather worse than the child's understanding of language. The probable explanation lies in a moderate impairment of non-verbal comprehension as verbal comprehension is appropriate to his level of mental development. Hearing will need to be measured. Indeed a general rule may be proffered, that whenever there is impairment of speech and/or language, audiological assessment is required routinely.

It is preferable to gain an adequate level of information and to delineate the child's disability within the constraints of a single visit. This is often forced on one because of the distances which the children travel quite apart from the natural anxiety of the parents. It has become the practice for assessment of the child to be carried out by physician and speech therapist working together in the same room with the parents present the whole time. The problems of these children can be immensely complex, and no one person working in isolation can hope to achieve very much, or to gain results of sufficient accuracy. It would be misleading if I were to give the impression that it is always possible to fill in the details of each major component in one visit. Some children are quite bewildering in the symptomatology and patterns of behaviour they show, and the problems they present on the diagnostic side alone tax one to the uttermost. Usually though, it is possible, and desirable also to have outlined the pattern of the child's disabilities, and to have measured his hearing threshold. A more precise delineation can be achieved during subsequent visits, often because parents make more information available in the course of these visits, and often alas as one corrects one's earlier errors.

Components Essential to Syndrome Delineation

In order to arrive at an adequate albeit very basic description of the child's disability of spoken language, it is necessary to add two further

TABLE 6

SYNDROMES IN ORDER OF MAGNITUDE
SHOWING NUMBERS OF CHILDREN

Order of magnitude	Number of syndromes encountered	Minimum size of syndrome	Total number of children (percentage of total in brackets)		Children: cumulative total (percent)
1	1	32	38	(12)	12
2	4	16	89	(28)	40
3	5	8	58	(18·5)	58·5
4	16	4	83	(26·5)	85
5	25	1	47	(15)	100

components to CA, NVC, VC and VX. These are Hearing (H) and
Speech (S). If each child is scored for each of the five on a three point
scale, the maximum number of combinations is 3^5, or 243. As we have
seen, a number of these simply cannot occur, and the question remains
— "How many are seen in practice?" Each combination of levels of
abilities may be thought of as a language disorder syndrome. Some of
these combinations or syndromes are seen frequently, some of them
less so, whilst others again may be represented by only one or two
children. In order to give due weight to the frequency of occurrence it
is helpful to think in terms of the magnitude of a syndrome, rather in
the way that the astronomer refers to the brightness of a star in magnitude terms.

The number of times a particular profile of disability occurred in the
present series is shown in Table 6. In the table the syndromes are
ranked in order of magnitude, with successive columns showing the
size, or minimum number of children who are allocated to each syndrome, the number of syndromes of that particular magnitude, the
number of children and the cumulative percentage. Nearly two-thirds
of the total number of children can be represented by 10 syndromes out
of a total of 51. Though this latter is a moderately large number it is a
considerable reduction from the theoretical maximum of 243. The ten
syndromes seen most frequently in this series, comprising the first
three orders of magnitude, are listed in Table 7.

If one looks at the first four, four very different patterns of disability
are seen. The most common was severe impairment of VC and VX,
with moderate impairment of S resulting from severe hearing loss, with
normal NVC. This clearly reflects the referral pattern to the department, and of course such findings as these cannot portray the true
prevalence of particular syndromes. It is perhaps surprising that the
next three syndromes show no evidence of hearing loss, and one can
begin to gain an impression of the likely pattern of distribution of
disability in the population as a whole. The second largest syndrome
shows moderately severe impairment of speech in the absence of any
other disability. This has interesting implications for the study of
neuromuscular control of the speech apparatus, and the children can
be broken down further into a series of more precisely defined patterns
of motor dysfunction. Clearly this component is a particularly vulner-

TABLE 7

First 10 syndromes ranked in order of magnitude

Syndrome magnitude	VC	NVC	H	VX	S	Number and percentage of children
1	2	0	2	2	1	38 (12.1)
2	0	0	0	0	1	29 (9.2)
	2	2	0	2	1	25 (7.9)
	0	0	0	2	1	19 (6.0)
	0	0	0	1	1	16 (5.1)
3	2	0	1	2	1	15 (4.8)
	0	0	1	0	0	14 (4.4)
	1	1	0	2	1	11 (3.5)
	2	1	0	2	1	10 (3.2)
	1	0	0	2	1	8 (2.5)

VC	verbal comprehension
NVC	non-verbal comprehension
H	hearing
VX	verbal expression
S	speech

0	normal range of ability
1	moderate impairment
2	severe impairment

able one in the developing child and the syndrome would be the greatest numerically in a truly representative sample. The third largest in the series is almost a mirror image of the first, with severe impairment of VC and VX, moderate impairment of S, with normal hearing, but severe overall mental retardation. The next syndrome shows impairment of expressive language, associated with moderate impairment of the functioning of the speech apparatus, but with normal non-verbal cognitive ability, normal hearing, and normal comprehension for spoken language thus ruling out any significant degree of auditory perceptual dysfunction. The nature and severity of so apparently specific a disorder of verbal expression demands a great deal of careful consideration, both in research terms and clinically. The greater number of children will almost certainly prove to have a complex neurolinguistic disorder, and we must be wary of labelling such children as emotionally disturbed. This is especially important because the inability to communicate with parents and peers induces intense emotional problems.

Conclusions

The accurate delineation of the child's pattern of language disorder is profoundly important. The nomenclature at the present time is both inadequate and imprecise, so that no two people agree on the exact meaning of any particular verbal formula for characterizing a syndrome or condition. What for instance does "specific developmental language delay" mean in real terms? Only when we know what we are referring to can we converse meaningfully about such vital issues as aetiology, the implications for disorders of genetic origin, or the exploration of subtle neurochemical malfunctioning. Accurate diagnosis hangs upon accurate delineation of the disability, and so does the planning and carrying out of the regime of therapy: the importance of this for the language disordered child and his parents needs no emphasis. There are further considerations to be borne in mind. Medicine is in a position to make useful contributions to the understanding of the normal processes of language learning, of the nature of auditory and speech perception, of the relationship between comprehension and the spontaneous verbal expression of thought, and of the encoding of complex motor processes.

References

Bayley, N. (1935) The development of motor abilities during the first 3 years, *Monogr. Soc. Res. Ch. Develop.,* **1**.

Bloom, L. (1970) *Language Development: Form and Function in Emerging Grammars,* M.I.T. Press, Cambridge, Mass.

Brown, R. (1973) *A First Language; The Early Stages,* Harvard University Press, Cambridge, Mass.

Bruner, J.S. (1975) The ontogenesis of speech acts, *Journal of Child Language,* **2**, 1–19.

Crystal, D., Fletcher, P. and Garman, M. (1976) *The Grammatical Analysis of Language Disorders: A Procedure for Assessment and Remediation,* Arnold, London.

Fourcin, A.J. (1978) Acoustic patterns and speech acquisition, pp. 47–72, In:

N. Waterson and C. Snow, (eds.), *The Development of Communication*, Wiley, Chichester.

Reynell, J. (1969) *Test Manual. Reynell Developmental Language Scales*, Experimental edition, National Foundation for Educational Research, Slough.

Sheridan, M. (1977) *Spontaneous Play in Early Childhood*, N.F.E.R., Slough.

Snijders, J. Th. and Snijders-Oomen, N, (1959) *Non-verbal Intelligence Test*, J.B. Walters, Groningen.

Wechsler, D. (1949) *Wechsler Intelligence Scale for Children*, The Psychological Corporation, New York.

Whitaker, H. A. (1976) Neurobiology of language, In: E. C. Carterette, and M.P. Friedman, *Handbook of Perception*, Vol. VII, *Language and Speech*, Academic Press, London, pp 121–44.

CHAPTER 5

A Follow Up of Speech Retarded Children

T. FUNDUDIS, I. KOLVIN AND R. F. GARSIDE*

Nuffield Psychology and Psychiatry Unit, Newcastle-upon-Tyne

Introduction

There have been few follow-up studies of children with delay of speech development which have attempted to assess outcome in a systematic and comprehensive manner. A unique opportunity to carry out this type of longitudinal follow-up occurred as a result of the Newcastle Child Development Study (Neligan *et al.*, 1974). In order to achieve this objective a series of preliminary simple steps were essential.

First, a definition of speech retardation: we decided to use the simple definition employed by the health visitors in the above study – *the failure to use three or more words strung together to make some sort of sense by the age of thirty-six months*. Admittedly this criterion is crude and arbitrary but it has the merit of being an objective, simple and standard way of recording a developmental milestone; it is, in fact, a crude screening technique which has to be followed by intensive assessment and diagnosis. Second, to select groups of children from a total population and to examine them at specified ages and by appropriate methods in order to identify the significant differences in their development. If such findings were to have more general validity it was essential for us to define the relationship between our study population and the total population from which it was drawn so that relevant

*Abstracted from *Speech Retarded and Deaf Children: Their Psychological Development* (1979) (T. Fundudis, I. Kolvin and R.F. Garside, Eds.) Copyright 1979 with permission from Academic Press and the Editors.

comparisons could be made and conclusions drawn by workers located elsewhere. Using a total population sample avoids the selection bias which besets clinic and hospital studies.

The Newcastle Survey of Child Development enrolled survivors of the first month of life born in Newcastle during the years 1960–1962 and our baseline was their 1962 cohort. This study gave us information, which has been collected by midwives, health visitors, doctors and teachers, about the children's first five years of life. This covered perinatal, obstetric and social data, and also information about their health and development. Descriptions of the population and other aspects of the study are provided in two previous monographs (Neligan *et al.*, 1974; Neligan *et al.*, 1976). Using a total population enabled us to study prevalence taking two factors into account:

(a)   Although the size of the population (3,300 children) was not large enough to produce reliable prevalence figures for relatively rare disorders, nevertheless, it provides a rough guide in an area where there is often little information.

(b)   Using a symptom as an ascertainment criterion does not ensure complete coverage of the disorders which it is meant to identify. This is because all children with such disorders do not necessarily have a speech delay of the severity defined by our criteria so that the prevalence figures reported provide only a conservative estimate.

The aim of the study was to obtain a comprehensive picture of the intellectual, behavioural and physical functioning of children at school age with an earlier history of speech retardation. It has been pointed out (Butler *et al.*, 1973) that seven years is a convenient age for assessment of speech and language defects because by then most of the developmental mispronunciations have disappeared spontaneously, and those that remain are either intrinsically serious or have serious implications.

The progress of the children with speech delay was compared with that of a matched control group. The latter consisted of children who did not suffer from speech delay and who were matched individually with our index cases on three criteria – sex, age and family neighbourhood. Of the 3,300 children born in Newcastle upon Tyne in 1962, 133 were identified as speech retarded. This constitutes 4 per cent of the population. Of these, 102 were studied more intensively when they were 7–8 years old.

Attrition

Thirty-one of the original 133 cases were not available for full testing at school age. Such losses constitute a potential source of bias so it is important to know how far the fully tested group are representative of the total cases identified as being retarded in speech at the age of three years. The distribution of the occupational social class of the families of these 31 children proved to be slightly higher and the rate of serious handicap no greater than in the group available for assessment (with the exception of the two children who had died). We therefore concluded that those children who were not seen were unlikely to differ significantly from those assessed at school age.

The initial screen was essentially to identify children who were speech retarded. The subsequent diagnostic assessment at 7 years identified those speech, language and other defects of which speech retardation is a symptom. This showed clearly that the cases could be divided into two broad groups.

The *first group* consisted of those whose functioning, intellectually, psychologically or physically, was so abnormal that we described them as pathological deviants. Such cases fall into three relatively well-defined clinical groups:

(a) *Marked Intellectual Impairment:* This was defined as an IQ at or below the 1st percentile on the WISC or where the child was untestable. In practical terms this meant an IQ of 65 or below. This is possibly too rigorous a criterion as other authors have used a criterion of 2 standard deviations below the mean, i.e. IQ of 70 or below (Yule and Rutter, 1970).

(b) *Specific Clinical Syndromes:* This included children with severe communication disorders of childhood, such as elective mutism (Salfield, 1950; *Brown et al.*, 1963); infantile autism (Creak, 1961; Rutter, 1968; Kolvin *et al.*, 1971) and cleft palate/dysarthrias or severe language disorders.

(c)   *Demonstrable Neurological Disorders:* This includes children with spastic disorders. These three categories were not intended to be mutually exclusive. For the purposes of this brief presentation we have classified disorders according to the most predominant feature. Finally, we decided that deafness alone should not constitute sufficient grounds for labelling the child pathologically deviant.

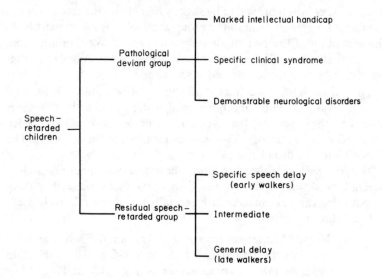

The *second group* consisted of children who, after clinical examination at the age of seven years, showed no evidence of serious handicap. We have labelled them the residual speech retarded group. More sophisticated psychological assessments were necessary to delineate their characteristics.

A further clinical classification was undertaken. This was dependent on whether these children suffered from speech retardation alone or whether they suffered from retardation of both speech and walking. In short, we identified three subgroups: those *who walked early* comprised the *specific speech delayed* group; those *who walked late* comprised the *general delayed* group; and those whose walking milestones were average comprised the *intermediate* group. In a later section we provide details of this classification.

The next problem was to reconcile the crude initial classification with a clinical classification of speech and language disorders. We decided to model our classification on the work of Ingram (1959 a; b; 1969; 1972). His is essentially a functional clinical classification and we have modified it both by abbreviation and simplification to suit our research as follows:

(a) *Dysarthria* – disorder of speech sound production with demonstrable dysfunction or structural abnormalities of tongue, lips, teeth or palate.

(b) *Secondary Speech Disorders* – disorder of speech sound production associated with other diseases or environmental factors.
  (i) Mental defect
  (ii) Hearing defect
  (iii) True dysphasia (acquired)
  (iv) Adverse environmental factors
  (v) Psychiatric disorders

Ingram (1972) points out that acquired dysphasia implies the loss of acquired language functions and therefore a birth-injured child cannot be described as having lost language functions, but more accurately as showing a retardation of speech and language development. If a child suffers serious brain insult at the age of two to three years there is likely to be both impairment of language and thereafter slowing of speech development.

Specific Developmental Speech Disorders (The developmental speech disorder syndrome):

(i) Mild (dyslalia)

(ii) Moderate (developmental expressive dysphasia)
(iii) Severe (developmental receptive dysphasia, word deafness)
(iv) Very severe (auditory imperception, central deafness)

Ingram (1972) sees the developmental speech disorder syndrome as a descriptive label given to children with retardation of speech development, who are otherwise apparently normal in respect of their health, intelligence and home backgrounds.

Ingram (1972) also points out that the label "Developmental speech disorder syndrome" is really a misnomer as the category comprises a heterogeneous group of articulatory and language disorders and in certain cases the speech development is not only retarded but deviant as well. He finds it useful to regard this category as a spectrum of disorders which varies from the mild to the very severe. The mildest are the dyslalias which are defined as "retardation of acquisition of word sounds but with normal language", i.e. the articulatory development of affected children is retarded. They are described by their parents as understanding the words but being unable to say them. Ingram also reports that the child substitutes or omits the later acquired consonants and consonant clusters inconsistently "though his vocabulary and grammatical structures in spoken language may be within normal limits." Children with moderate developmental speech disorders have normal comprehension but more severe retardation of word sound acquisition and retardation of development of spoken languages. The severely affected children have greater degrees of retardation of word sound acquisition, impaired development of spoken language and impaired comprehension of speech. Synonyms for these three degrees of severity are "dyslalias", developmental expressive dysphasia and developmental receptive dysphasia, respectively.

It will be seen that included in our pathological deviant category are Ingram's dysarthrias and secondary speech disorders. Our "residual speech retarded" group comprised the remainder of the children. One could argue that these fall into the developmental speech disorder syndrome provided we widen Ingram's inclusive criteria to cover as well the dull range of intelligence and without stipulating a normal home background. It remains to be seen whether characteristic features of the syndrome can be identified clinically or statistically.

Milestones and the Specificity of Speech Retardation

As previously stated, our criterion for speech retardation was a delay in using three-word sentences by thirty-six months. This corresponds to the third percentile based on Neligan and Prudham's (1969) norms for developmental milestones. We defined walking retardation as onset of walking occurring below the tenth percentile (using Neligan and Prudham's norms) which in practice meant grouping of children according to whether they were walking before or after 16 months. A child was therefore considered to have a general delay in milestone achievement if he was retarded in speech and in addition had not walked yet unsupported by 16 months. Next, we identified a group of children who were retarded in speech but walked early, i.e. had a specific speech delay. For this purpose early walking was defined as onset of walking occurring above the 75 percentile (according to Neligan and Prudham's norms) i.e. at or below 12 months. The above method identifies three groups:

(a) Specific developmental speech delay, i.e. a group of 25 children who walked early but were speech retarded. Using the above criteria the minimal rate is about 8 per 1,000 children.

(b) An intermediate group of 34 (who were speech retarded but walked by 16 months).

(c) General milestone delay, i.e. a group of 23 children who walked late and also were speech retarded. Using the above criteria the minimal rate is again about 8 per 1,000 children.

Some Background Factors – Residual Speech Retarded Group

(i) Sex ratio

While the population sex ratio in Newcastle approaches unity (Neligan, Scott and Kolvin — personal communication) that of our speech retarded group was 1.7 boys to 1 girl. This is roughly consistent with the ratio reported in most studies of developmental disorders where the ratio of boys to girls is in the order 2:1 to 3:1.

When the residual speech retarded group and the pathological deviants are analysed separately, the ratio is 2:1 for the former, and 1:1 for the latter. This leads to the preliminary conclusion that the sex ratio of the former group resembles that described in developmental disorders. Rutter *et al.* (1970) report that there is a tendency for biological and perinatal hazards to occur more frequently among young males than females, with the inevitable consequence that a higher number of boys than girls subsequently are handicapped. In addition there is a greater vulnerability of boys to environmental stress (Neligan *et al.*, 1976.)

(ii) *Perinatal factors*

The mean gestational ages of the pathological deviant group and also the residual speech retarded group were significantly lower than that of the controls. This finding is similar to that described by Butler *et al.*, (1973) in children with speech defects. However, in contrast to the Butler study, we found that our total speech retarded group had a significantly lower birth weight than did the controls.

(iii) *Birth Order*

The mean family size reveals a trend for the residual speech retarded to come from larger families (chi-squared = p < .05). In addition it was found that fewer of the speech retarded group were first born.

(iv) *Other milestones*

We also found that the residual speech retarded group achieved bladder control and unsupported walking later than the controls, but this was statistically significant for walking only. This means that our residual speech retarded group is, on the average, less retarded on walking than on speech. Possible explanations for this are provided elsewhere (Fundudis *et al.*, 1979).

(v) *Laterality*

There were no significant differences in terms of right, mixed or left-handedness between the controls and the speech retarded group; nor were there any significant differences in the number of right, mixed or left-eyed children between the group. The only significant differences concerned confusion in differentiating between the left and right side of the body; the speech retarded children were significantly worse in this respect.

Faulty cerebral dominance has been incriminated as the basis of developmental language disorders (Orton, 1937; 1934). However, in a recent survey of the literature (Rutter *et al.*, 1970), it was found that reports of excess of left and/or mixed laterality in speech retarded children tend to be highly contradictory with "as many reports of negative findings as of positive findings." This is not unexpected, as most of the previous studies have been mainly clinic or hospital populations.

Prevalence of Speech Retardation at the Age of Three

At the age of three years we found 4 per cent (133) of 3,300 children had retardation of speech as reported by health visitors. This is a lower percentage than that described in the 1,000 Family Study (Spence *et al.*, 1954; Morley, 1965) where a 6 per cent retardation is described at the same age using broadly similar criteria. It is of importance to note that in the 1,000 Family Study about 1 per cent were still using incomplete sentences just before starting school, but 4 per cent remained unintelligible at time of entry into school.

Prevalence of Disorders at Follow-up

Of the 102 speech retarded children studied at the age of seven 18 fell into the pathological deviant category. For simplicity the cases in the sub-categories are presented as mutually exclusive in the first column in Table 1. The second column contains overlap cases and hence the sum of frequencies is greater than 18 (see Table 1).

TABLE 1
Incidence

Pathological deviant group

(categorised according to predominant disorder)   n = 18

		Predominant	Total
A.	Marked intellectual handicap alone	7	13
B.	Cerebral palsy	5	5
C	Specific syndromes:		
	Autism	2	2
	Elective mutism	2	2
	Severe dysphasia	1	1
	Cleft palate dysarthria alone	1	2

Residual speech-retarded group   n = 84

(includes two deaf children with no other demonstrable handicaps)

			Total	n = 102

Pathological Deviant Group

(i) *Infantile Autism:* We found two cases with characteristic autism.

(ii) *Elective Mutism:* We recorded only two "nuclear" electively mute children (Tramer, 1934) with an inordinate and selective shyness of strangers severe enough to persist into the seventh year of life. Elective mutism would therefore appear to be as rare a condition as infantile autism.

(iii) *Dysphasia:* Problems of definition confound frequency and prevalence studies of childhood dysphasia. Some use both verbal behaviour and presumed aetiology as diagnostic criteria whereas others use verbal behaviour alone (Ingram and Reid, 1956; Morley, 1965; Lenneberg, 1967; Eisenson, 1968). Even though one can theoretically make the distinction between an acquired dysphasia (Ingram, 1972) and the moderate or severe form of the specific developmental speech disorder syndrome (Ingram, 1972) which some would label as developmental expressive or developmental receptive dysphasia respectively, in practice we found the distinction difficult because of the part retrospective nature of the research diagnostic exercise. In fact, we uncovered only one case which could be included in the clear-cut severe dysphasic category. Our figures therefore support the suggestion that the condition is as rare or even rarer than infantile autism.

(iv) *Dysarthria:* While Morley (1965) reports one case of cleft palate per 1,000 births, we found two per 3,300 children.

(v) *Deafness, Hearing Impairment:* Deafness is one of the major causes of delay in speech and language development (Morley, 1965). It has been estimated (Pless and Graham, 1970) that about 2 per 1,000 children have deafness severe enough to merit the use of hearing aids, but those with severe hearing loss are even less than this. We found 2 profoundly deaf children and a further 2 with less severe forms of deafness but with associated multiple handicaps. This leads to a rate similar to those reported by Barton *et al.*, (1962); Reed (1970) and Neligan *et al.*, (1974) in the major Newcastle survey of which this study forms a part. As the two cases presenting with only profound deafness and language retardation showed little in the way of other signs of handicap, we decided for the purposes of analysis not to include them in the pathological deviant group.

(vi) *Cerebral Palsy:* Our 5 cases of cerebral palsy gives rise to a rate which closely approximates that reported by Neligan *et al.* (1974) in the major survey of which our study forms a part.

(vii) *Intellectual Handicap:* We found 7 cases of marked intellectual handicap alone although some 13 children had both severe intellectual handicap and other associated handicaps. The rate, therefore, is about 5.1 in 1,000. If we employ the criterion of a performance IQ of 70 or less then the numbers marginally increase to 14 and the rate becomes 5.5 per 1,000.

The Residual Speech Retarded Group

(i) *Prevalence*

It will be remembered that these comprise the remainder of the children who did not fall into the category of being "pathologically deviant". If we make no qualification about intelligence or home background (provided we exclude children with severe intellectual handicap) these children could be considered as falling into Ingram's (1972) specific developmental speech disorder syndrome. This gives rise to a prevalence rate of 2 to 3 per cent of children of school age.

(ii) *Cognitive, Language and Educational Development*

We have made no attempt in our study to use the newer linguistic concepts or to explore factors such as the rules of grammar and language competence (Chomsky, 1969). Like Mittler (1970), we believe that these measures are still clinically in their infancy and need highly specialised skills for their application. Instead, we have used traditional clinical psychological measures such as the Illinois Test of Psycholinguistic Abilities (Kirk *et al.*, 1968, revised edition), together with a wide range of other standard measures for assessing language development.

The residual speech retarded group scored significantly poorer than the *controls* on all the *cognitive* (intelligence, perceptual, conceptual and visualmotor abilities) and language tests. This applied equally to the *global test* scores and to the *subtest* scores. Full details of statistical and other findings are reported in our main publication (Fundudis *et al.*, 1979). The initial interpretation of these results is that the poorer functioning of the residual speech retarded group reflects wider intellectual impairment. On the other hand, it may well be that the residual speech retarded group is not really a homogeneous group and therefore the above analyses may have masked patterns of abilities specific to particular subgroups. We therefore divided the residual speech retarded group according to the classification previously described. In summary, our groups consist of early walkers who we have labelled the specific speech delayed group, late walkers who we have labelled the general delayed groups and an intermediate group whose walking milestones fell between the two extremes.

An analysis of the cognitive and language development of each of these three groups at the age of seven years reveals that the functioning of all of them is depressed in relation to the controls (Table 2). First, the early walkers (i.e. the group with a specific delay in speech) have significantly poorer verbal IQ, language ability and educational achievements compared to the controls. In contrast, however, their non-verbal IQ compares very favourably with that of the control group. This pattern is similar for the intermediate group but not so for the late walkers (i.e. the general delayed group). The latter group not only perform poorly on all the above measures but also score significantly poorer on performance IQ than do the controls.

TABLE 2
Cognitive functioning at follow up

Tests	Controls = C	Residual speech-retarded: Early walkers = E	Inter walkers = I	Late walkers = L	C vs. E	C vs. I	C vs. L
Verbal							
IQ – WISC	93	85	84	81	1%	1%	1%
Non-verbal							
Performance IQ – WISC	101	99	98	87	N.S.	N.S.	1%
Language							
ITPA-Quotient	91	84	82	76	1%	1%	1%
Achievements							
Reading Quotient Schonell	94	82	81	76	1%	1%	1%

A similar pattern was found on other cognitive measures which we have used and details are available elsewhere (Fundudis *et al.*, 1979). In brief the early walkers, with one exception, do as well as the controls on non-verbal tests, but again do consistently worse on verbal and language tests. The late walkers do significantly worse than the controls even on non-verbal tests.

Discussion

Awareness of the long-term sequelae of speech retardation is of paramount importance. There is evidence (Morley, 1965) that the frequent use of incomplete sentences at the age of 3 years 9 months rapidly improves, so that one year later very few children have this disability. Further, Butler *et al.* (1973) point out that by the age of 7 years most developmental mispronunciations have disappeared spontaneously. Such apparent spontaneous improvement does not necessarily mean that henceforth all will be well, as there are reports of worrying long term consequences. For example, the Edinburgh research group (Ingram, 1963; Mason, 1967), in their follow-up of speech retarded children in primary schools, report that the majority have reading difficulties. In addition, Rutter (1972) points out that to read and "to understand the meaning of what he reads . . . a child must have language skills". He accordingly argues that speech delayed children are likely to have reading delays as well because both reflect language impairment. Our findings suggest that speech delay is a better predictor of impaired verbal intelligence than of performance intelligence; and that a combined delay in speech and walking is a good predictor of poor cognitive, language and educational development. We have other evidence to demonstrate that at the age of seven, the three subgroups of speech retarded children have residual linguistic difficulties. The extent of the difficulties is closely tied to their previous prowess or delay in walking.

Summary

Our results emphasise the predictive value of a simple speech screen at the age of 3 years. About 1 in 5 of the 4 per cent of all children aged 3 years who were speech retarded were later found to have serious language, intellectual or physical handicaps. This underlines the value of an early screening exercise (Butler *et al.*, 1973) in identifying children with handicaps who may need more intensive assessment or help with appropriate placement. What must be emphasised, however, is that what happens at 3 does not reflect the total position at 5, 6 or 7 years, so that a comprehensive screening programme should include periodic re-examination over the first 5 to 7 years of life. If the extreme group (pathological deviant group) is set aside, it was commonly assumed that the children in the residual group would soon overcome their speech disability and thereafter will function normally in most respects. Our follow-up study at school age of previously speech retarded children reveals widespread impairments and in this way expands on the findings of other workers (Ingram and Reid, 1956; Mason, 1967) who have shown that a high percentage of such children later develop educational disabilities. In this chapter we describe some of the residual cognitive, language and educational deficits of these children. A comprehensive account of cognitive, speech, language, educational, physical, social and behavioural outcome is provided elsewhere (Fundudis *et al.*, 1979).

Acknowledgements

Details of acknowledgements are provided elsewhere. We would, however, like to acknowledge our main co-authors — Mrs. G.S. George, Dr. H.I.J. van der Spuy, Mrs. J.S.H. Nolan and Mrs. E. Scanlon. In addition we are indebted to Mrs. M. Blackburn for administrative and secretarial help.

References

Barton, M.E., Court, S.D. and Walker, W. (1962) Causes of deafness in school children in Northumberland and Durham, *British Medical Journal*, 1, 351–55.

Browne, E., Wilson, V. and Laybourne, P.C. (1963) Diagnosis and treatment of elective mutism in children, *Journal of American Academy of Child Psychiatry*, 2, 605–17.

Butler, N., Peckham, C. and Sheridan, M. (1973) Speech defects in children aged 7 years: a national study, *British Medical Journal*, 1, 253–57.

Chomsky, N. (1969) *The Acquisition of Syntax in Children from 5 to 10*, M.I.T. Press, Cambridge, Mass.

Creak, E.M. (1961) Schizophrenic syndrome in childhood: progress report of a working party (April, 1961), *Cerebral Palsy Bulletin*, 3, 501–4.

Eisenson, J. (1968) Developmental aphasia (dyslogia): A postulation of a unitary concept of the disorder, *Cortex*, 4, 184–200.

Fundudis, T., Kolvin, I. and Garside, R.F. (1979) *Speech Retarded and Deaf Children: Their Psychological Development*, Academic Press, London.

Ingram, T.T.S. (1959a) A description of classification of common disorders of speech in childhood, *Archives of Disease in Childhood*, 34, 444–55.

Ingram, T.T.S. (1959b) Specific developmental disorders of speech in childhood, *Brain*, 82, 450–67.

Ingram, T.T.S. (1963) Delayed development of speech with special reference to dyslexia, *Proceedings of Royal Society of Medicine*, **56**, 199–203.

Ingram, T.T.S. (1969) Developmental disorders of speech. In: P. J. Vinken and W. Bruin (eds.), *Handbook of Clinical Neurology*, Vol. 4, Amsterdam, North Holland.

Ingram, T.T.S. (1972) The classification of speech and language disorders in young children *In:* M. Rutter and J.A.M. Martin (eds.), *The Child with Delayed Speech,* Clinics in Developmental Medicine No. 43. Heinemann Medical Books Ltd., London.

Ingram, T.T.S. and Reid, J.F. (1956) Developmental aphasia observed in a department of child psychiatry, *Archives of Disease in Childhood*, **3**, 161–72.

Kirk, S.A., McCarthy, J.J. and Kirk, W.D. (1968) *Examiners Manual: Illinois Test of Psycholinguistic Abilities* (revised edition), University of Illinois Press.

Kolvin, I., Ounsted, C., Humphrey, M. and McNay, A. (1971) The phenomenology of childhood psychoses, *British Journal of Psychiatry*, **118**, 385–95.

Lenneberg, E.H. (1967) *Biological Foundations of Language*, John Wiley & Sons, New York.

Mason, A.W. (1967) Specific (developmental) dyslexia, *Developmental Medicine and Child Neurology*, **9**, 183–90.

Mittler, P.J. (1970) Language Disorders. *In:* (P. Mittler (ed.) *The Psychological Assessment of Mental and Physical Handicaps,* Methuen, London.

Morley, M. (1965) *The Development and Disorders of Speech in Childhood*, Second Edition, Churchill Livingstone, London.

Neligan, G. and Prudham, D. (1969) Norms for four standard developmental milestones by sex, social class and place in family, *Developmental Medicine and Child Neurology*, **11**, 413–22.

Neligan, G., Prudham, D. and Steiner, H. (1974) *The Formative Years: Birth, Family and Development in Newcastle upon Tyne*, Nuffield Provincial Hospitals Trust, Oxford.

Neligan, G., Kolvin, I., Scott, D. McI. and Garside, R.F. (1976) *Born Too Soon or Too Small*, Clinics in Developmental Medicine No. 61, Heinemann Medical Books Ltd., London.

Orton, S.T. (1934) Some studies in the language function, *Res. Publ. Ass. Res. Nerv. Ment. Dis.*, **13**, 614–33.

Orton, S.T. (1937) *Reading, Writing and Speech Problems in Children*, Chapman and Hall, London.

Pless, B. and Graham, P. (1970) Epidemiology of physical disorder. *In:* M. Rutter, J. Tizard, and K. Whitmore, (eds.), *Education, Health and Behaviour*, Longman, London.

Reed, M. (1970) Deaf and partially hearing children, *In:* P. Mittler, (ed.) *The Psychological Assessment of Mental and Physical Handicaps,* Methuen, London.

Rutter, M. (1968) Concepts of autism: a review of research, *Journal of Child Psychology and Psychiatry*, **9**, 1–25.

Rutter, M. (1972) The effects of language delay on development. *In:* (Rutter and J.A.M. Martin, (eds.) *The Child with Delayed Speech,* Clinics in Developmental Medicine No. 43, Heinemann Medical Books Ltd., London.

Rutter, M., Graham, P. and Yule, W. (1970) *A Neuropsychiatric Study in Childhood*, Clinics in Developmental Medicine No. 35/36, Heinemann Medical Books Ltd., London.

Rutter, M. and Mittler, P. (1972) Environmental influences on language development,

In: M. Rutter, & J.A.M. Martin, (eds.) *The Child With Delayed Speech,* Clinics in Developmental Medicine No. 43, Heinemann Medical Books Ltd., London.

Salfield, D.J. (1950) Observations of elective mutism in children, *Journal of Mental Science,* **96**, 1024–32.

Spence, J.C., Walton, W.S., Miller, F.J.W. and Court, S.D.M. (1954) *A Thousand Families in Newcastle upon Tyne*, O.U.P., London.

Tramer, M. (1934) Electiver Mutismus bei Kindern, *Z. Kinderpsychiat.,* **1**. 30–35.

Yule, W. and Rutter, M. (1970) Intelligence and educational attainment of children with psychiatric disorder, *In:* M. Rutter, J. Tizard, and K. Whitmore, (eds.), *Education Health and Behaviour,* Longmans, London.

CHAPTER 6

The Home Treatment of Autistic Children

PATRICIA HOWLIN

Psychology Department, Institute of Psychiatry, London

Language Deficits in Autistic Children

In his original writings on early childhood autism, Kanner was impressed particularly by the language handicap shown by autistic children. This was, he wrote, characterised by "either mutism or the kind of language which does not seem intended to serve the purpose of interpersonal communication. An analysis of this language has revealed a peculiar reversal of pronouns, neologisms, metaphors and apparently irrelevant utterances" (Kanner, 1949).

The failure to develop normal communication skills has since been accepted as one of the most important features in the diagnosis of autism. Abnormalities of language are often reported by the parents of autistic children as being the first problems to give concern. The autistic child typically fails to take part in the reciprocal "pre-linguistic conversations" which normally develop between mothers and children (Lewis and Freedle, 1973; Olson, 1970), and he neither responds to, or initiates verbal or social interactions. The development of babble, too, is likely to be affected (Ricks, 1975). The babbling sounds made by autistic children are rarely as extensive as the range of sounds made by normal infants, and the speech cadences which usually develop as a child approaches his first birthday do not appear.

This work was supported by a generous grant from the DHSS from 1970–1977, and was a collaborative study with R. Hemsley, M. Berger, L. Hersov, D. Holbrook, M. Rutter and W. Yule.

115

Many autistic children remain mute, and in those who do learn to talk the acquisition of language is usually very delayed. Even when speech does appear it may not be used to communicate, but frequently comprises meaningless and repetitive utterances.

The development of language skills is closely related to outcome and follow-up studies indicate that unless some use of spontaneous language is achieved by the age of 5 or 6 years prognosis is likely to be poor, even in children who show a relatively high level of non-verbal skills (Eisenberg, 1956; Rutter, 1966; Brown, 1960; De Meyer *et al.*, 1973; Lotter, 1974). The extent of the language handicap in autism is also related to the general severity of the disorder and to the child's response to treatment (Rimland, 1964; Fish *et al.*, 1968; Davis, 1967).

Although language delay was originally considered to be only one of the many symptoms associated with autism, more detailed studies of the nature of the language handicap suggest this is not the case. Work by Rutter *et al.* (1971) and Ricks and Wing (1975) indicates that the language and cognitive deficit is, in fact, basic to the disorder, and that problems such as impaired social relationships, rituals and obsessions and many behaviour problems arise *because* of the child's inability to understand or make himself understood.

The Treatment of Language Problems

The severity of the language handicap in autism, and the importance of language development for outcome has led to a search for ways of ameliorating the problem. In recent years, operant approaches, using a combination of prompting, modelling, and reinforcement techniques have been increasingly used to develop language and communication skills in autistic children.

Since the original studies of Lovaas *et al.* (1966) there have been numerous reports in the literature of the use of operant techniques in developing language. Many of these studies, however, have been single case reports, lacking in satisfactory baseline data, follow-up assessments or experimental controls. Even in those studies which do involve groups of children experimental design is often far from adequate. Diagnostic data and cognitive and linguistic assessments on the children concerned are frequently lacking, despite the fact that these may have important implications for outcome. Training programmes tend to have been limited to a few, somewhat arbitrarily chosen aspects of language and little heed has been taken of the importance of relating language programmes to the child's general cognitive development.

Moreover, most training has been carried out by professional therapists in a clinic setting, although reports by Browning (1971) and Lovaas *et al.* (1973) indicate that the beneficial effects of language training may be short-lived unless parents, or the child's usual caretakers, are actively involved in treatment.

Description of the "Home-Based" Project

In the present study, which was designed to evaluate the effectiveness of behavioural techniques, we attempted to overcome at least some of these problems. All children were diagnosed according to the criteria of Rutter (1971) and were assessed fully on psychometric and language tests before and after treatment. The children involved in treatment consisted of 16 boys between the ages of 3 and 11. Control groups of untreated children matched for age, IQ level and general severity of disorder were used to assess the effectiveness of treatment over time.

Two separate control groups were used. The first comprised a group of mothers and autistic children who were assessed on similar measures to the experimental group on 2 occasions, 6 months apart. No intervention with these families took place over this period. Changes in the language-interaction between control mothers and children were then compared with changes in the language interaction of the experimental group after the first 6 months of treatment. The second control group consisted of a group of children individually matched with experimental cases for age, IQ and severity of behavioural and language disorder when first seen at the Maudsley Hospital. These children were compared with the experimental group at final follow-up.

Treatment programmes were individually designed for each child, and in addition to language deficits, many other behaviour problems, such as obsessions, rituals, phobias, temper tantrums, and overactivity were also treated. Details of these training programmes may be found in Howlin *et al.* (1973), Marchant *et al.* (1974) and Hemsley *et al.* (1978).

All training was carried out by parents in the home and intervention lasted for 18 months. Visits to the home by the therapists to collect data and advise on training programmes were made weekly for the first 6 months and were then gradually faded to once or twice a month.

The Design of Language Training Programmes

The methods used to develop expressive and receptive language skills were based on those described by Lovaas (1966), Sloane and MacAulay (1968), Bricker and Bricker (1970) and Yule and Berger (1972).

At the onset of treatment parents were trained in basic techniques, such as prompting appropriate responses, correcting incorrect utterances and reinforcing the child's attempts to use, or respond to language. They were asked to set aside short periods a day, of between 10 and 15 minutes, when training new concepts or structures. In addition they were encouraged to respond warmly and consistently to any spontaneous utterances made by the child during the rest of the day, no matter how simple these were, and to attempt to elicit appropriate verbalisations from the child whenever the opportunity arose.

In collaboration with the parents individual language programmes were designed for each child. These were based on all available information from psycholinguistic research and the linguistic structures used were those which are known to be acquired early by normal young children, and which were commensurate with the child's general cognitive level. If carried out rigorously language training can prove to be extremely arduous and time consuming. It is essential, therefore, in order to avoid frustration and disappointment, to ensure that programmes are carefully tailored to the needs and abilities of each particular child. If a programme proved unsuccessful for an individual child we did not persist with this but modified the training procedures until they proved more effective. We did not, as in some projects, follow a predetermined programme regardless of results. Lovaas (1977) for example, reports that over 90,000 trials were needed to teach one child to use two simple word labels. Few parents would have the stamina to continue training for such meagre returns, and, anyway, this would hardly seem to be a particularly economical way of teaching language.

Individual Training Programmes: The Development of Comprehension

It became obvious, fairly early in the course of the project that certain children were unlikely to profit, at least to begin with, from attempts to improve their expressive language.

If a child had little or no comprehension of spoken language and made few spontaneous sounds, attempts to teach him to copy sounds, or increase the range of his vocalisations were almost invariably unsuccessful. Such children did benefit, however, from programmes to increase their understanding of speech. By the careful use of prompts and physical guidance or gestures, together with consistent reinforcement for their co-operation, children were taught to associate spoken commands with particular actions. Simple instructions such as "Sit" or "Stand up" would be introduced initially, with physical prompts and gestures being gradually withdrawn until the child was able to respond to the spoken instruction alone.

Progress in the early stages of training tended to be slow and arduous, the first few commands often taking many weeks to acquire. Thereafter, however, learning seemed to progress more rapidly and parents were then able to go on to teach the child to understand many different words and more useful, everyday instructions.

It is important in these early stages of training to ensure that the instructions worked on are ones which are frequently heard by the child, so that he has constant opportunities for relating the spoken words with the appropriate actions. It is also important that all those involved in the child's care are involved in training if the outcome is to be more generally successful. Work with autistic children has shown that generalisation to other situations or to other people cannot be expected to occur automatically (Baer *et al.*, 1968). Generalisation, too, must be planned for. If it is not, skills learned in one setting will not necessarily appear in others. Figure 1, for example, shows the number of words and commands learned by a young, non-speaking boy at home. After slow progress initially, these increased considerably over a period of a year. At school, however, where there was little emphasis on language development progress remained very limited.

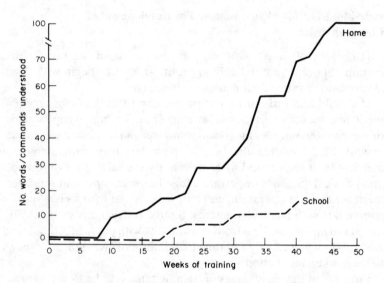

FIG. 1   Comprehension Training in 5-Year Old Boy.

It was noticeable, during the course of the project, that when a child first learned to respond to simple instructions, the relationship between him and his parents often began to improve dramatically. Perhaps for the first time, parents were able to control the child's actions through speech and the child himself was able to make a little sense of the language heard around him. This frequently resulted, according to parents' reports, in a marked increase in sociability and a corresponding decrease in tantrums and obsessional and ritualistic behaviours.

Expressive Language Training: The Development of Imitation

Once a child is able to respond to simple commands and makes a few sounds spontaneously, training in expressive skills can begin. Kinaesthetic training, using physical guidance, can be used to teach the child how to form his mouth into the correct shape and how to emit particular sounds (Nelson and Evans, 1968; Nelson *et al.*, 1976). Open vowel sounds such as "oo" or "aah" which are easy to demonstrate and to prompt physically are usually the first to be attempted. At first any effort which the child makes to produce the sounds should be warmly rewarded, but gradually, at the same time as physical prompts are reduced, the child should be rewarded only for closer and closer approximations to the sounds made by the therapist.

When the child is able to imitate a number of sounds without difficulty, training should focus on teaching him to link these together to form simple words or word approximations. For example, if the sounds "K" and "Ah" are in the child's repertoire, he can be taught to chain these together to form an approximation to the word "car". If he can make single sounds such as "Ma" or "Da", these, too, can be run together to make approximations to "Mama" or "Dada" in order to gain his parents' attention more easily.

By this stage in training it is important that all the child's "words" are associated with familiar objects. Imitation for the sake of imitation, is of little value. The objects used should be those which the child has the opportunity of seeing and naming everyday. They should also be, whenever possible, items which the child particularly likes so that his attempts at naming can be reinforced by his actually obtaining the object. If the child learns that all his attempts at naming, no matter how primitive, always meet with a positive response, whereas simply screaming or pointing vaguely in the direction of what he wants is ignored, his motivation to use speech is likely to be increased. Again, usually the first words are acquired slowly, but gradually the rate of acquisition increases. Figure 2 shows the development of vocabulary in a 3½ year old boy. Although initially mute when treatment began, by the time he was admitted to school, 9 months later, his expressive language age as measured by the Reynell Language Scales (Reynell,

1969) was only slightly below his chronological age.

Progress in older children tended to be less dramatic, but vocabulary did increase steadily. Figure 3 shows rate of acquisition in a 7 year old boy, and this illustrates too, the need to ensure that treatment is carried out in all relevant situations. Although his use of words continued to increase gradually at home, he showed much less progress at school, where again there was little emphasis on the development of language. Similarly during a period spent in hospital, when training was discontinued, no increase in vocabulary occurred.

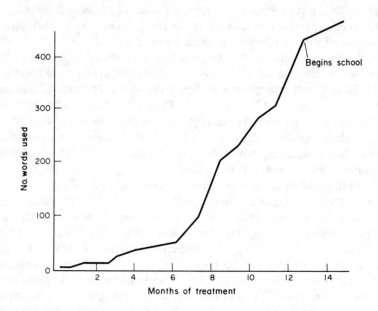

FIG. 2   Development of Expressive Vocabulary in 3-Year Old Boy.

Increasing Spontaneous Language

Once the child has developed a fairly extensive labelling vocabulary, it is important to build up his spontaneous use of nouns to ask for and

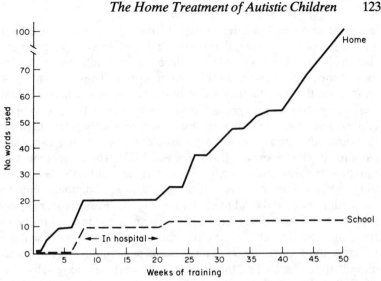

FIG. 3   Training Expressive Vocabulary in 7-Year Old Boy.

talk about everyday objects and to answer simple questions. Other parts of speech can then be introduced. The use of verbs allows the child to describe his own actions and those of others around him. The use of simple adjectives can also help to increase his descriptive skills. Whatever new speech forms are taught these should always be introduced in the same gradual way: prompting the child to imitate the correct word and rewarding his attempts, then gradually reducing prompts until he is able to use the words spontaneously.

When the child is using many single words these can be chained together to form simple phrases such as Noun + Verb, or Adjective + Noun, and to increase the flexibility of his language, simple morpheme and transformational rules can be taught.

The Acquisition of Language "Rules"

Although there is some controversy as to whether language in handicapped children follows the same developmental patterns as language in normal children (Menyuk, 1969; Lenneberg *et al.*, 1964; Freedman and Carpenter, 1976) the weight of evidence seems to suggest that the linguistic rules acquired easily by normal children are also the easiest for language delayed children to acquire. Thus, in training we worked on those semantic relationships which tend to appear in children's early phrases, i.e.: possessives (Johnny's shoe), Locatives (In the cup), Agent + Action (Mummy sleep), Action + Object (Hit ball) and demonstrative and attributive phrases (That book, Big car, etc)., (Slobin, 1970; Bowerman, 1973; Brown, 1973). The morpheme rules taught were also those which appear early in children's speech: the "ing" ending of the present progressive ("running", "jumping" etc.) the "s" ending on plurals and possessives ("cups", "Mummy's" etc.) and simple verb tenses. Structures which are known to present problems for young normal children before the age of 4 or 5 were avoided (Clarke and Clarke, 1977). Thus, use of prepositions was restricted initially to "in" and "on" the pronoun "it" was taught long before "I" or "You". Many relational terms such as "Give and Take", "Come and Go", "Big and Small" etc. were omitted until the child had reached the appropriate mental age for dealing with such structures. Transformations taught were again those which were normally acquired early, such as the use of the "imperative" and "question" forms.

One of the major criticisms of operant approaches to language training is the suggestion that all such programmes achieve is to teach children to "parrot" what they hear more effectively. Even amongst behaviour-therapists themselves, doubt has been expressed as to whether such techniques can produce more than simple associative learning (Weiss and Born, 1967).

However, a number of studies, mainly with mentally retarded children, have shown that it is possible for children to be taught simple linguistic rules which they are then able to generalise to novel utterances (Guess *et al.* 1974).

In the present study, after children had begun learning specific rules, their ability to generalise these rules to other, untaught structures was assessed. Although rule generalisation had to be taught initially, rather than appearing spontaneously, in most children it did occur eventually. Figure 4 for example, shows a child's use of the singular and

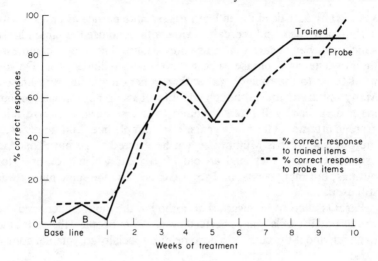

FIG. 4   Use of Singular and Plural Verb Forms During Training

plural forms of the verb "to be" in trained and untrained probe sentences.

Evidence of generalised rule learning was also apparent in the errors made by the children and many children made the mistake, which is typical of normal children, of *over*-generalising rules (e.g. goed, wented, sheeps, etc; Cazden, 1968). Some children even began to inflect their own neologisms appropriately!

Decreasing Inappropriate Speech

As well as the need to increase communicative speech there was the need to *decrease* certain types of utterance in a number of children. Occasional echolalia, or repetition of other's speech, is common in the speech of young normal children around the age of two, but in autistic children echolalia is often much more prolonged and extensive. Many autistic children learn to associate particular phrases with certain activities, and thereafter will continue to use the same phrase which they have heard others use previously. Thus, they will indicate their own needs by phrases such as "Do you want dinner?" or "Do you want to go to the toilet?" rather than generating their own phrases. Many children, too, although capable of using appropriate, grammatical speech, will often continue to use somewhat bizarre telegraphic utterances for many years. For example one child simply used the phrase "Morris Mummy" when he wanted to go out. This had originated when they had an old Morris car which they used for outings, but many years, and several cars later, the same phrase was still used.

Parents need to be aware that, although they may understand the child's odd use of language perfectly well, other people will not be able to do so, and if the child is to become more socially acceptable, appro-

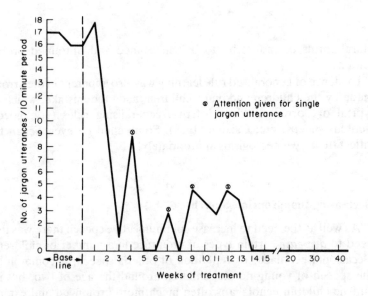

FIG. 5   Extinction of Jargon Utterances in 7-Year Old Boy.

priate use of speech is important. Some parents, having lived so long with a child who did not talk, are reluctant to begin correcting him when he does so; others may no longer even notice how bizarre their child's speech may appear to others. However, if echolalic or stereotyped utterances are consistently corrected, and if only appropriate phrases are responded to, rates of echolalia tend to decrease rapidly and are accompanied by a concomitant increase in appropriate socialised speech.

Occasionally echoed or jargon utterances may be used deliberately by a child to gain attention, and if this occurs, totally ignoring the use of such phrases is generally the best policy. Figure 5 shows the extinction, by ignoring, of jargon usage in a 7 year old boy. He came from a poor West Indian family in which the mother's main aim was to keep things clean and tidy. The only two-word phrases which this child used, began always with the word "Dirty" (as in Dirty Baby, Dirty Mummy, Dirty Carpet etc.), the one adjective calculated to throw Mother into the most ferocious rages. Despite constant and severe beatings the use of such phrases seemed, if anything, to be increasing. Not until this Mother agreed to ignore them completely did they begin to decline. He then managed to think up new, and equally infuriating phrases from time to time. These invariably met with an outburst of rage from mother, with the consequence that they increased again rapidly. Eventually, however, she learned to ignore such phrases fairly successfully, and since then the use of these utterances has almost entirely disappeared.

Increasing Socialised Responses

The development of socialised speech also involved teaching the child to use so-called "Automatic" or "Intraverbal" utterances (Jackson, 1932; Skinner, 1957). These include responses such as "Please", "Thank you", "How are you", "Yes, No" answers to questions and other conversational "rituals" which are typically lacking in the speech of autistic children. Such responses are postulated as being represented in the non-dominant hemisphere of the brain (Van Lancker, 1975), and although the teaching of these responses does not necessarily improve the child's syntactic or semantic development, they are important in enabling the child to appear more socially acceptable.

The social naivity of autistic children often means that even when they have learned to talk, they still need to be taught when it is, or rather when it is not appropriate to talk about particular topics. It can be very confusing for a child who having been encouraged for years to talk *more*, suddenly finds himself scolded for what he does say.

The complexities of social interactions are such that it is impossible to teach the child the multitude of rules involved. However, they can be taught simple rules, such as not to talk to strangers, not to mention certain topics in public, or to talk quietly if they are commenting on what other people are doing. The concept of "whispering" rather than talking in a normal voice can be very difficult for some children to grasp. One mother tried to overcome this by teaching her son to talk as if he were in the library. He now asks loudly, "Do I have to talk like I was in the library?" before launching into somewhat vituperative comments about the lady sitting in front of him on the bus!

Alternative Forms of Communication

Of the 16 experimental children in the study, thirteen, three of whom were initially mute, showed considerable improvements in their use of communicative speech. Moreover, although not all children developed spoken language, all showed improvements in their understanding of language, and all but one developed some mode of communication. One child for example, who made few sounds but who imitated gestures readily, was taught a simple sign language. Another child with virtually no comprehension of speech, but with excellent non-verbal skills, learned to associate written words first with objects and then with pictures. He was then able to respond to quite complex written instructions such as "Get the big blue ball" or "Fetch Susie's coat" or "Go to the toilet" etc. He would also use cards to communicate his desire for certain things, mostly of an edible kind, such as "Pudding" or "Fruit". In both these children training in an alternative mode of communication, far from inhibiting their understanding of spoken language actually seemed to enhance it. Many other studies, too, have recently shown that if a child fails to develop speech, training in other forms of communication may eventually result in the spontaneous development of verbal skills (De Villiers and Naughton, 1971; Fulwiler and Fouts, 1976; Deich and Hodges, 1977).

The problem involved in teaching alternative forms of communication is in being able to identify, at an early stage, those children who are most likely to benefit from training in non-verbal systems, thereby avoiding possibly months of frustration and disappointment spent in fruitless attempts to train verbal skills. More large scale studies, and more details of the children who do, and do not respond to verbal training programmes are needed before early decisions can be made about the most appropriate modes of training for individual children.

The Development of Play

Language, of course, does not involve only direct communicative skills; the capacity for symbolic thought and abstract reasoning is also an integral part of language development. Initially, in normal children, imaginative and symbolic abilities are externalised, manifesting themselves in "pretend" games and activities. These early imaginative games are important in the later growth of "inner language" and symbolic thought. Children who are severely retarded in their imaginative play are usually also severely handicapped in language ability, and in autistic children symbolic activities and imaginative play do *not* develop spontaneously. In an attempt to lay down the rudiments of symbolic play, children were deliberately taught how to play with toys: how to dress and undress dolls, to put them to bed and to offer them "pretend" cups of tea, and so forth. Such activities meant little to most children at first but gradually many came to enjoy them. Several children now show simple spontaneous pretend play, such as inventing families of dolls from scraps of material and talking to them as if they were real. These activities are usually rather limited and do not involve elaborate imaginative games with other children. Nevertheless, the growth of symbolic play in the children studied was closely associated with their development in other areas of language and social skills.

The Outcome of Treatment – Short-Term Results

As well as monitoring progress in individual children, group comparisons were used to assess the general effectiveness of treatment techniques.

TABLE 1
Functional speech analysis

Echolalic or autistic utterances
Immediate Echolalia
Self-repetition
Delayed echoes
Inappropriate remarks
Action accompaniments
Thinking aloud
Metaphorical utterances

Socialised utterances
Prompted responses
Commands
Questions
Answers
Spontaneous remarks
Other (reading, counting, etc.)
Exclamations

Other
Non-verbal
Incomprehensible

At the end of the first 6 months of home intervention, language development in the experimental children was compared with that in control children. Children were assessed according to the amount and type of speech they used (Table 1) and on the syntactic complexity of their utterances (Table 2) (see Cantwell *et al.*, 1977 for further details of measures used). Assessments were based on ½ hour tape recordings of the verbal interaction between children and their mothers at home, since this relatively short period of time had been found to give a reliable estimate of language use over much longer periods (Howlin *et al.*, 1973(b). Mothers were also assessed according to how much they talked to their children, and how much of their speech was used to

TABLE 2
Analysis of language level

Phrase-level
Complex sentences
Simple sentences
Phrases
Mean morpheme length of utterance

Morphemes
Present progressive /ing/
3rd person singular /s/
3rd person regular past /ed/
3rd person irregular past
Plural /s/
Possessive /s/
Pronouns + case
Prepositions
Articles
Adverbial & adjectival inflections

Transformations
Imperative
Question-inversion
Wh-question
Negation
Auxiliary
Copula
"Do" – support

elicit language from the child (Table 3) (All categories used in the assessment of mothers' and children's speech were of a high level of reliability. Cantwell *et al.* 1977; Howlin *et al.*, 1973(b).

Before treatment began cases and control were very similar in their use of language. Control children used rather more appropriate and spontaneous speech initially, and the complexity of their utterances was somewhat greater than in the cases but there were no significant differences between the groups. However, over the first 6 months experimental children almost doubled the amount of speech they used during the observation period. There were significant increases in the proportion of socialised utterances they used and significant reductions in their use of non-verbal utterances. There was also a decrease in echolalic and stereotyped utterances, although this difference fell

TABLE 3
Mothers' speech analysis

Language eliciting utterances
Questions
Answers
Imitations
Expansions
Reductions
Prompts
Corrections
Reinforcement

Non-language directed utterances
Directions
Statements
Approval
Disapproval
Indirect modelling (story-telling etc.)

Other
Interjections
Incomprehensible

---

short of statistical significance (Table 4). In other words, not only did they begin to speak more, but they also came to make a greater use of speech for social communication.

In sharp contrast the control children failed to show change on any of these measures, and the pattern of their speech remained very stable over 6 months.

Changes in grammatical complexity were less marked. Controls were rather more advanced than cases (although not significantly so) before treatment and remained so at the end of 6 months. The gap between the two groups narrowed considerably during the course of treatment, but no significant changes occurred (Table 5).

Change in Mothers' Speech

Assessment of the speech used by mothers in the experimental and control groups over 6 months showed changes similar to those found in

TABLE 4

Changes in children's use of language over 6 months:
comparison between cases and short term controls

	Cases				Controls			
	Initial assessment		6 months assessment		Initial assessment		6 months assessment	
	Mean	SD	Mean	SD	Mean	SD	Mean	SD
Total number of utterances	89.5	(102.4)	190.4***[2]	(112.5)	130.3	(134.5)	171.2	(162.9)
% Socialised	30.8	(25.1)	49.1*	(30.7)	43.2	(32.0)	42.3	(25.7)
% Autistic/echolalic	18.0	(15.9)	11.8	(12.6)	11.9	(15.0)	16.0	(17.8)
% Non-verbal[1]	57.1	(36.3)	37.9*	(41.3)	58.7	(42.2)	56.4	(37.3)

1* % of non-verbal utterances based on mean for all children. Other categories include speaking children only.

2* = significance of change over 6 months.

*   = p > .05
*** = p > .005

TABLE 5

Changes in children's level of language over 6 months:
comparison between cases and short term controls[1]

| | Cases | | | | Controls | | | |
| | Initial assessment | | 6 months assessment | | Initial assessment | | 6 months assessment | |
	Mean	SD	Mean	SD	Mean	SD	Mean	SD
Number of correct sentences	14.7	(33.2)	23.9	(34.7)	28.0	(30.1)	33.4	(40.4)
Number of correct phrases	32.1	(64.3)	58.9*[2]	(73.4)	60.6	(62.7)	77.0[1]	(74.4)
Number of Morphemes	54.1	(116.5)	106.4*	(117.8)	123.5	(118.3)	129.5	(133.6)
Number of transformations	27.9	(61.3)	54.8*	(78.5)	68.5	(70.9)	85.6	(96.6)

[1]Figures based only on children using some phrase speech.

[2]Significance of change over 6 months.

* = p > .05

the children. Control mothers showed virtually no change over the 6 month period whereas mothers in the experimental group showed many improvements. Compared to the initial assessment they were talking far more to their children (Table 6) and using far more utterances designed to encourage their children's speech. There was also a highly significant correlation (rho = + .72) between mothers who showed most improvement in their use of language–eliciting utterances, and increase in socialised speech in children. That is, mothers who changed most had children who changed most.

The Longer-Term Follow-Up: Children's Language

After the 6 month assessment, experimental children were again assessed 6 months later and at the end of treatment.* The improvements which occurred in the first 6 months were maintained over the final year of treatment, despite a reduction in therapist intervention over this time. Increases in the frequency of children's utterances and in their use of communicative speech continued, although the rate of change slowed down a little (Fig. 6). Grammatical complexity on the other hand showed less improvement (Fig. 7). It had been hoped, following the rather disappointing results of the first 6 months that changes in grammatical structure, being more complex than changes in *use* of language might simply respond more slowly to treatment and that longer periods of training would be more successful. However, after the relatively small changes in the first 6 months, the complexity of children's utterances showed little further change. It seemed therefore that while treatment was extremely effective in teaching children to use language in an appropriate and useful way it was less successful in developing complex language skills.

Comparisons with the long-term control group also supported this finding. The children in this group had all been matched with cases for age, sex, severity of disturbance etc., when they were first seen at the

---

* The untreated control group was not used in these subsequent measures since it was felt unethical to request them to continue to co-operate with the lengthy assessment procedures without offering help and advice in return.

TABLE 6

Changes in mother's language over 6 months:
comparison between cases and short-term controls

| | Cases | | | | Controls | | | |
| | Initial assessment | | 6 months assessment | | Initial assessment | | 6 months assessment | |
	Mean	SD	Mean	SD	Mean	SD	Mean	SD
Total number of utterances	253.6	(113.0)	407.5**	(149.6)	309.6	(123.1)	286.8	(144.2)
% language eliciting	25.8	(18.1)	45.7***	(23.8)	33.0	(17.1)	36.6	(16.1)
% non language eliciting	64.8	(16.6)	48.1**	(22.3)	56.4	(17.1)	49.7	(16.6)
% interjections/ incomprehensible	9.2	(4.6)	6.2	(4.2)	10.7	(5.7)	13.4	(6.4)

* Significance of change over 6 months.

** = p > .01
*** = p > .005

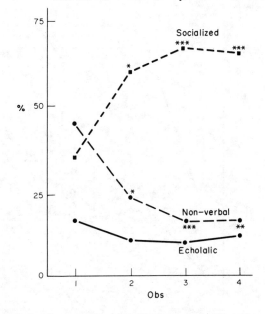

FIG. 6   Changes in Functional Language over 18 months.

* = Significance of change between 1st and subsequent occasions.

    *= $p < .05$
   **= $p < .01$
  ***= $p < .005$

Analysis of Variance Data Show Significant Linear Trends in Amount and Use of Socialised Speech.

Maudsley. In the interim period they had occasional outpatient contacts with consultants at the Maudsley and parents had been given similar advice to experimental parents concerning treatment and management. They had not, however received intensive care at home. At follow-up these children were somewhat older than cases (average length of time between first clinic assessment and follow-up was 63 months for controls, 33 months for the experimental group) a fact which led to problems in the analysis of results. However, using statistical regression techniques to take into account the effects of age it

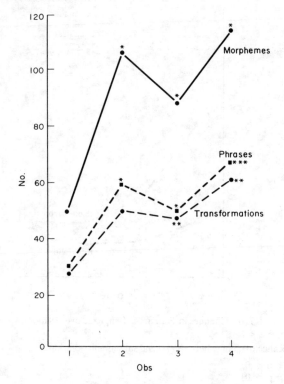

FIG. 7   Change in Language Level over 18 Months

* = Significance of change between 1st and subsequent occasions

$$* = p < .05$$
$$** = p < .01$$
$$*** = p < .005$$

was found that improvement was greater in cases than controls although the difference did not reach statistical significance. On measures of functional language cases were superior to controls despite being younger, but on measures of language complexity, although cases achieved a higher level than predicted, there was less difference between cases and controls (Table 7).

TABLE 7

Longer term follow-up of language in cases and controls

Spontaneous Language	Cases		Controls		Significance of Difference
	Mean	SD	Mean	SD	t-value
Number of utterances	217.5	(103.2)	175.5	(118.7)	1.15
% socialised	69.4	(23.4)	54.9	(31.7)	1.12
% echolalic/autistic	12.8	(8.9)	10.6	(11.4)	0.63
% non-verbal	33.1	(38.0)	46.8	(39.7)	0.94
Number of phrases	88.0	(61.9)	78.1	(77.5)	0.95
Number of morphemes	115.4	(90.8)	150.3	(118.6)	0.87
Number of transformations	61.4	(74.2)	54.6	(97.6)	1.01
Reynell Language Scales					
Expression age	32.4	(21.2)	38.9	(27.6)	0.58
Comprehension age	37.4	(18.7)	46.5	(21.3)	0.84

Numbers of non-verbal utterances and scores on Reynell based on all children.
Scores in other categories based only on children using communicative/phrase speech.
t scores based on differences in regression equations taking into account disparity in age between the groups at follow-up.

Mothers' Speech

Over 18 months, mothers, too, maintained the early improvements in their speech to their children. There was a slight decrease in improvement after the first 6 months of treatment, possibly because of the reduction in therapist intervention at this time, but in the final 6 months the rate of change increased once more (Fig. 8).

Again, there was a high, positive correlation between change in mothers and changes in their children. Improvements in children's appropriate speech were *not* correlated with increases in the amount of mother's speech but rather with the proportion of language–eliciting remarks used, thereby indicating that it is not how much mothers say, but *what* they say which is important.

Correlational data cannot, of course, be used to infer causal relationships, but there is at least circumstantial support for the assumption that changes in maternal language resulted in improvements in their children's speech rather than vice versa. Firstly, studies of operant language training have shown clearly that contingent reinforcement, used in conjunction with prompting and modelling, does result in improvements in language handicapped children (Lovaas *et al.* 1966, 1967). Secondly, in almost all cases, mothers showed increases in such utterances *before* the improvements in children's speech were recorded.

Obviously the relationship between changes in mothers' and children's speech is not a simple one – since as children's verbalisations become more frequent mothers have greater opportunity for reinforcing them – but it seems probable that the initial increases in children's utterances were due to mothers' deliberate attempts to elicit more appropriate speech.

Conclusions

The results of the project raise a number of interesting points. Firstly it is clear from the 6 month case-control comparisons that advice and help to parents at home does result in rapid improvements in children's communicative speech, improvements which are maintained even when therapist intervention is greatly reduced. Comparisons with the

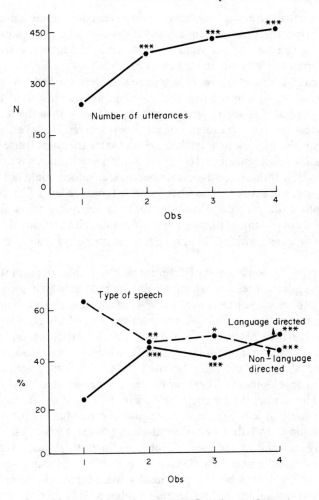

FIG. 8   Changes in Mother's Speech over 18 Months.

*   = significance of change between 1st and subsequent occasions

Analysis of Variance Data Show Significant Linear Trends in Frequency and Styles of Speech to Children.

long term control group also indicate that intervention at home is more successful than the usual system of outpatient contacts, even though the advice given may be very similar. However, although such treatment is apparently of value in increasing children's use of language to communicate, changes in level of language were less marked.

It is possible, of course, that the training programmes used for increasing syntactical ability were simply less effective than the techniques used to increase frequency of socialised speech. However, the findings can also be viewed as lending support to the theory of Rutter *et al.* (1971) that the linguistic and cognitive impairment in autism is basic to the disorder. If this were the case, operant techniques would not be expected to result in marked improvements in language level. Certainly throughout the project behaviour problems invariably responded more rapidly to treatment than problems of communication, and those aspects of language which did improve were in *use* rather than level of language.

The varying responsiveness of different children is also important in the interpretation of results. On the whole, the children who improved most were those who already used a few words or echolalic utterances when treatment began. The children who made least progress were those who had little comprehension of language, little spontaneous use of sounds or gestures, and who were particularly impoverished in their play (even though they might be highly skilled in other areas of non-verbal development). These results seem to suggest that the children for whom operant language programmes are most successful already possess at least some of the cognitive pre-requisites for language learning, and that behavioural methods are responsible for motivating such children to use their inherent linguistic abilities. If the basic cognitive skills needed for language acquisition are lacking – as in the case of children who are profoundly handicapped in comprehension, expression, and other language related skills such as play – operant techniques to train verbal communication are unlikely to be successful. In other words, behavioural methods would seem to be of most value in increasing children's linguistic *performance*, they apparently have less effect on more fundamental aspects of language *competence* (Chomsky, 1966).

References

Baer, D. M., Wolf, M.M. and Risley, T.R. (1968) Some current dimensions of applied behavior analysis. *J. Applied Behavior Analysis*, **1**, 91–97.

Bowerman, M. (1973) Structural relationships in children's utterances: syntactic or semantic? *In:* T. E. Moore (ed), *Cognitive Development and the Acquisition of Language*, Academic Press, New York, pp 197–213.

Bricker, W.A. and Bricker, D.D. (1970) Development of receptive vocabulary in severely retarded children, *Am J. Mental Deficiency*, **74**, 599–607.

Brown, J.L. (1960) Prognosis from presenting symptoms of pre-school children with atypical evelopment, *Am. J. Orthopsychiatry*, **30**, 383–90.

Brown, R. (1973) *A First Language: the early stages*. George Allen and Unwin, London.

Browning, R.M. (1971) Treatment effects of a total behaviour modification program with ive autistic children. *Behaviour Research and Therapy*, **9**, 319–28.

Cantwell, D. Howlin, P. and Rutter, M. (1977) The Analysis of language level and language function: a methodological study, *Brit. J. Disorders of Communication*, 119–35.

Cazden, C. (1968) The acquisition of noun and verb inflections. *Child Development*, **39**, 433–48.

Chomsky, N. (1966) *Aspects of the Theory of Syntax*, M.I.T. Press, Cambridge Mass.

Clark, H. and E.V. (1977) *Psychology and Language: An introduction to Linguistics*, Harcourt Brace, New York.

Davis, B.J. (1967) A clinical method of appraisal of the language and learning behaviour of young autistic children, *J. Communication Disorders*, **1**, 266–96.

De Haven, E.D. and Garcia, E.E. (1974) Continuation of training as a variable influencing the generalisation of speech in a retarded child, *J. Abnormal Child Psychology*, **3**, 217–27.

Deich, R. and Hodges, P. (1977) *Language without Speech*, Souvenir Press, London.

De Meyer, M.K. (1976) Motor, perceptual motor, and intellectual disabilities of autistic children, *In:* L. Wing (ed.), *Early Childhood Autism*, Second Edition, Pergamon, Oxford, pp 169–93.

De Meyer, M.K., Barton, S., De Meyer, W.E., Norton, J.A., Allan, J. and Steele, T. (1973) Prognosis in autism: a follow-up study, *J. Autism & Childhood Schizophrenia*, **3**, 199–246.

DeVilliers, J.G. and Naughton, J.M. (1974) Teaching a symbol language to autistic children, *J. Consulting Clinical Psychology*, **42**, 111–17.

Eisenberg, L. (1956) The autistic children in adolescence, *Am. J. Psychiatry*, **112**, 607–12.

Fish, B. Shapiro, T. Campbell, M. and Wile, R. (1968) A classification of schizophrenic children under 5 years, *Am. J. Psychiatry*, **124**, 1415–23.

Freedman, P. and Carpenter, L. (1976) Semantic relations used by normal and language impaired children at stage I. *J. Speech and Hearing Research*, **19**, 748–95.

Fulwiler, R.L. and Fouts, R.S. (1976) Acquisition of American sign language by a non-communicating autistic child, *J. Autism & Childhood Schizophrenia*, **6**, 43–51.

Guess, D., Sailor, W., and Baer, D.M. (1974) To teach language to retarded children, *In:* R.L. Schiefelbusch & L.L. Lloyds (eds.), *Language Perspectives — Acquisition, Retardation and Intervention*, MacMillan, London, pp. 529–63.

Hemsley, R., Howlin, P., Berger, M., Hersov, L., Holbrook, D., Rutter, M. and Yule,

W. (1978) Treating autistic children in a family context, *In:* M. Rutter and E, Schopler (eds.) *Autism: Reappraisal of Concepts and Treatment.* Plenum, New York, pp. 379–411.

Howlin, P.A., Cantwell, D., Marchant, R., Berger, M. and Rutter, M. (1973) Analysing mothers' speech to young children: a study of autistic children, *J. Abnormal Child Psychology,* 1, 317–39.

Howlin, P., Marchant, R., Rutter, M., Berger, M., Hersov, L. and Yule, W. (1973) A home-based approach to the treatment of autistic children. *J. Autism and Childhood Schizophrenia,* 4, 308–36.

Jackson, J.H. (1932) On the nature of the Duality of the Brain, *In:* J. Taylor (ed.), *Selected Writings of John Hughlings Jackson,* Mouton, The Hague, pp 156–60.

Kanner, L. (1943) Autistic disturbances of affective contact. *The Nervous Child,* 2, 217–50.

Lenneberg, E.H., Nichols, I.A. Rosenberger, E.F. (1964) Primitive stages of language in mongolism, *Disorders of Communication, Vol. XLII,* Research Publications A.R.N.M.D., pp. 119–39.

Lewis, M. and Freedle, R. (1973) Mother-infant dyad: the cradle of meaning. *In:* P. Liner, L. Krames and T. Alloway (eds.), *Communication and Affect: Language and Thought,* Academic Press, New York., pp. 350–64.

Lotter, V. (1974) Factors related to outcome in autistic children, *J. Autism & Childhood Schizophrenia,* 4, 263–77.

Lovaas, O.I. (1966) A program for the establishment of speech in psychotic children, *In:* J.K. Wing (ed.) *Early Childhood Autism: Clinical Educational and Social Aspects,* Pergamon Press, Oxford, pp. 115–44.

Lovaas, O.I. (1967) Behavior therapy approach to the treatment of childhood schizophrenics, *In:* J. Hill (ed.), *Minnesota Symposia on Child Psychology,* 1, 108–59, University of Minnesota Press, Minneapolis.

Lovaas, O.I. (1977) *The Autistic Child: Language Development Through Behavior Modification,* Wiley, New York.

Lovaas, O.I. Berberich, J.P., Perloff, B.F. and Schaeffer, B. (1966) Acquisition of imitative speech in schizophrenic children, *Science,* 151, 705–7.

Lovaas, O.I. Kogel, R. Simmons, J.Q. and Stevens, J. (1973) Some generalisations and follow-up measures on autistic children in behavior therapy, *J. Applied Behavior Ananlysis,* 6, 131–65.

Marchant, R., Howlin, P., Yule, W. and Rutter, M.L. (1974) Graded change in the treatment of the behaviour of autistic children, *J. Child Psychology and Psychiatry,* 15, 221–27.

Menyuk, P. (1969) *Sentences Children Use,* Research Monograph No. 52, M.I.T. Press, Cambridge Mass.

Nelson, R.O. and Evans, I.M. (1968) The combination of learning principles and speech therapy techniques in the treatment of non-communicating children, *J. Child Psychology and Psychiatry,* 9, 111–24.

Nelson, R.O., Peoples, A., Hay, L., Johnson, T. and Hay, W. (1976) The effectiveness of speech training techniques, based on operant conditioning: A comparison of two methods, *Mental Retardation,* 14, 34–37.

Olson, D.R. (1970) Language acquisition and cognitive development, *In:* H.C. Haywood (ed.), *Social-cultural Aspects of Mental Retardation.* Appleton Century Crofts, New York, pp. 257–73.

Reynell, J. (1969) *Reynell Developmental Language Scales,* N.F.E.R., Windsor,

England.

Ricks, D.M., (1975) Vocal communication in pre-verbal normal and autistic children, *In:* N. O'Connor (ed.), *Language, Cognitive Defecits and Retardation,* Butterworths, London, pp. 75–80.

Ricks, D.M. and Wing, L. (1975) Language, communication and the use of symbols in normal and autistic children, *J. Autism and Childhood Schizophrenia,* **5,** 191–221.

Rimland, B. (1964) *Infantile Autism,* Appleton Century Crofts, New York.

Rutter, M. (1966) Prognosis: Psychotic children in adolescence and early adult life, *In:* J.K. Wing (ed.), *Early Childhood Autism: Clinical Educational and Social Aspects,* Pergamon, London, pp. 83–100.

Rutter, M. (1971) The description and classification of infantile autism, *In:* D.W. Churchill, G.D. Alpern and M.K. De Myer (eds.), *Infantile Autism,* Charles C. Thomas, Springfield, Ill.

Rutter, M., Bartak, L. and Newman, S. (1971) Autism — A central disorder of cognition and language? *In:* M. Rutter (ed.), *Infantile Autism; Concepts, Chracteristics and Treatment,* Churchill, London, pp. 148–71.

Skinner, B.F. (1957) *Verbal Behavior,* Appleton-Century-Crofts, New York.

Sloane, H.N. and MacAulay, B.D. (1968) *Operant Procedures in Remedial Speech and Language Training,* Houghton Mifflin, Boston.

Slobin, D.I. (1970) Universals of grammatical development in children. *In:* G.B. Flores d'Arcais and J.W. Levett (eds.), *Advances in Psycholinguistics,* North Holland Press, Amsterdam, pp. 174–186.

Van Lancker, D. (1975) Heterogeneity in language and speech: neurolinguistic studies, *Working Papers in Phonetics,* U.C.L.A., No. 29.

Weiss, H.H. and Born, B. (1967) Speech training or language acquisition? A distinction when speech is taught by operant conditioning procedures, *Am. J. Orthopsychiatry,* **37,** 49–55.

Yule, W. and Berger, M. (1972) Behaviour modification principles and speech delay, *In:* M.L. Rutter and J.A.M. Martin (eds.), *The Child with Delayed Speech, Clinics in Developmental Medicine, No. 43,* Spastics International Medical Publications, William Heinemann, London, pp. 204–19.

Yule, W. and Berger, M. (1975) Communication, language and behaviour modification, Reprinted from: *Behaviour Modification with the Severely Retarded. Institute for Mental and Multiple Handicap, Study Group 8,* pp. 35–65.

CHAPTER 7

Language training
with autistic children:
How does it work
and what does it achieve?

MICHAEL RUTTER

Department of Child & Adolescent Psychiatry, Institute of Psychiatry, London.

Patricia Howlin (Chapter 6) has described how a variety of behavioural techniques may be used to aid the development of spoken language in autistic children. Examples were given of cases in which training was associated with marked gains in vocabulary, syntax and socialised speech usage. Experimental-control group comparisons showed that the improvements in language tended to be greater in the treated children. The results are encouraging and indicate the value of a behaviourally oriented home based treatment programme for autistic children (see Hemsley *et al.*, 1978 and Rutter *et al.*, 1977 for fuller accounts of what was achieved by this treatment approach). The demonstrated advantages and achievements of this therapeutic approach are sufficient to recommend it as a worthwhile method for general adoption. However, many questions, both theoretical and practical, remain. In this paper, I will focus on just two issues concerned with the language training element in the programme – namely the questions of *how* does training work and *what* does it achieve? In order to answer these questions it is necessary both to consider our own findings in greater detail and to review what is known from other studies on language acquisition and the language deficits of autistic children.

Language Disorders in Autistic Children

In considering the problem to be treated we need to examine in detail the nature of the autistic child's linguistic deficits. The first point is that the language delay is part of a broader cognitive disorder which involves impaired coding, sequencing, conceptualisation and abstraction (Hermelin and O'Connor, 1970; Bartak *et al.*, 1975, 1977).

Second, autistic children lack imaginative play and imitative skills, and their language impairment involves *all* modalities, not just speech. Thus, they also have difficulties in gesture and in written language, (Bartak *et al.*, 1975). Not only are they severely impaired in language comprehension but also the receptive difficulty tends to be unusually persistent. The expressive problem involves not just the use of words but also the expression of ideas (Cantwell *et al.*, 1978). The language problem of autistic children stands out from other language disorders in being more severe, more extensive and more persistent.

Third, as well as a delayed development of language there is an impairment in its social usage. Compared with other children of comparable linguistic maturity, autistic children are less likely to use language spontaneously for social communication (Bartak *et al.*, 1975; Cantwell *et al.*, 1978). The basis and nature of this social deficit remains obscure but it is a very persistent feature of autistic language.

Fourth, autistic children's spoken language is not only immature, it is also grossly deviant (Bartak *et al*, 1975; Cantwell *et al.*, 1978). Delayed echoes, thinking aloud or action accompaniments, and inappropriate echoes of themselves are especially characteristic.

Fifth, the cognitive deficit in autism is biologically, not motivationally, determined (Rutter, 1979). This is shown by the pattern of cognitive test performance (Clark and Rutter, 1977, 1979), by the experimental evidence of impaired memory and thought processes (Hermelin and O'Connor, 1970), by the association between low IQ and the development of epileptic fits (Bartak and Rutter, 1976), and by the genetic findings from twin studies (Folstein and Rutter, 1977).

In short, the problem is not just the aiding of language development in a child with linguistic impairment. The language delay is associated with language deviance and forms part of a broader cognitive deficit of biological origin. Moreover, the language difficulties are associated with a multiple of social and behavioural problems (Rutter, 1978).

TABLE 1
Longer term follow-up of behavioural measures in cases and controls

Parental Interview data	Cases		Controls(b)		Significance	
	Mean	(SD)	Mean	(SD)	t	(p value)
Language deviance/delay	34.1	(33.0)	41.8	(33.4)	0.65	N.S.
Social deviance	10.9	(4.7)	18.2	(6.7)	3.56	(< 0.005)
Abnormal response to parents	1.8	(1.9)	4.8	(3.1)	3.33	(< 0.005)
Social disruption	4.6	(2.9)	7.0	(3.5)	2.13	(< 0.05)
Abnormal peer relationships	4.6	(1.2)	6.5	(1.9)	3.49	(< 0.005)
Stereotyped play	13.5	(8.6)	20.8	(10.9)	2.09	(< 0.05)
Obsessions and rituals	4.6	(4.0)	10.6	(5.4)	3.59	(< 0.005)
Behavioural abnormalities	4.8	(3.9)	10.8	(7.6)	2.82	(< 0.01)

Results of the Home-Based Programme

Patricia Howlin has already given the main findings on the results of the home-based treatment programme but it is necessary to bring out a few additional features. First, the long-term case-control comparison on the information derived from parental interviews* shows that the treatment was much more successful in dealing with the social, emotional, and behavioural problems of autistic children than it was in aiding normal language development. On all measures except language the cases were *much* better off at follow-up. With respect to language deviance, the cases had also done better than controls but the difference fell short of statistical significance.

TABLE 2

Child by child comparisons on long term follow-up of language skills
(after partialling out effects of time)

Measures	Cases superior to matched long term controls	Cases inferior to matched long term controls
Number of comprehensible utterances	11	5*
Number of socialised communicative utterances	11	5*
Number of correct phrases	10	6
Number of morphemes	10	6
Number of transformations	13	3**
Reynell Expressive Language	9	7
Reynell Language Comprehension	9	7

$*X^2 = 3.12; p < 0.05$ $**X^2 = 6.12; p < 0.01$

Second, autistic children's improvements in language were generally rather more impressive with respect to social usage than to linguistic competence. Thus, on a case by case comparison, after partialling out the effects of different lengths of follow-up, 11 out of 16 autistic children were superior to their controls in terms of socialised

*The extent of the children's deviance was assessed through the use of detailed interview schedules covering many different aspects of play, social skills, language development and behavioural disorder. A scale was created for each category of abnormality, based on the number and severity of abnormal features.

communication (a difference significant at the 10 per cent level). But on the Reynell (1969) scales, only 9 cases were superior and 7 were worse.

This long-term comparison emphasises the need for control groups in any evaluation of the effects of behavioural treatments on a developmental function (Kazdin, 1973). All 16 autistic children had improved with treatment to some extent, making the results quite impressive when each child was used as his own control. However, the gains were put into a different perspective by the finding that many of the controls had also greatly improved. Of course, their improvement was not necessarily "spontaneous" in that they, too, had received some treatment. But their treatment had been much less intense than that given

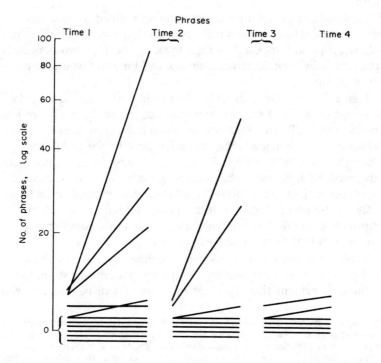

FIG. 1

to the cases and in some instances it had been extremely sporadic and infrequent.

The third point about the results is the *huge* individual variation. Figure 1 shows the results on our measure of phrase structure (see Cantwell *et al*, 1977 for details) for children with initially poor language skills (i.e. less than 10 phrases during a ½ hour audio-taped session with the mother at home) at the beginning of each of the follow-up periods*. Of the 7 children with no measurable grammatical skills when we first saw them, *six* remained without skills 6 months later. The pattern for changes in the second and third 6 months periods of follow-up were much the same. A few mute children made remarkable gains but on the whole they did very badly. On the other hand, *most* of those with just a little language made tremendous gains with treatment.

This was the group for whom treatment seemed to have most to offer. It should be noted that the reason why improvements in the third follow-up period appear less than those in the first two periods is simply that by then there was only one child in this favourable prognostic group.

Figure 2 shows the findings for the children who started with more language in each of the follow-up periods. Here the gains are less consistent. At all three time periods about half the children improved and about half remained the same (a few actually got slightly worse). Over the 18 month period all but one of these linguistically more advanced children made substantial progress but the response to treatment seemed less direct. However, although not included on the figure it should be noted that even if this group did not make such steady improvement in their use of syntax they *did* improve considerably and consistently in their social usage of language.

Table 3 summarises the prognostic findings. In this case the cases and controls have been pooled because the pattern was so similar in both. It is evident that the great majority of autistic children who

---

*The figure is organised according to the child's initial language level at the start of *each* following period, in order to indicate the effect of initial level. Thus, children who improved during the first 6 months period so that they were using more than 10 phrases at the beginning of the second 6 months period were excluded from this Figure and instead were included on Figure 2.

TABLE 3
Language development in cases and controls

Initial language level	No. of children*	Level at follow-up: Nos. of Children							
		Mute		Words/word approximations		Simple phrases		Good phrase speech	
		Cases	Controls	Cases	Controls	Cases	Controls	Cases	Controls
Mute	12	2	3	2	3	1	0	1	0
Words/word approximations	4			0	2	1	0	1	0
Spontaneous words + Echolalia	12					1	2	5	4
Spontaneous phrase speech	4							2	2

* Cases and controls were matched for language level initially so half the children in each group are cases, half are controls.

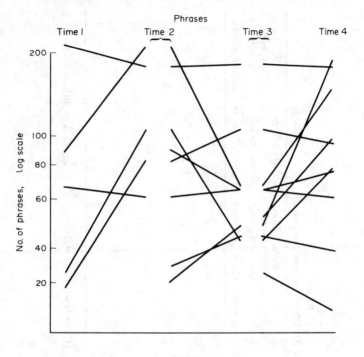

FIG. 2

started mute either remained mute or gained only isolated words. (It should be noted that most of the children were over 4 years of age and obviously the same would not apply to much younger children who have to start by being without speech!). In sharp contrast, of the children who started with either echolalia or spontaneous words, most gained good phrase speech. Clearly, the initial level of language is of great prognostic importance.

The findings from other studies are closely comparable. For example, in Lovaas' sample (Lovaas *et al.*, 1973) of 13 treated autistic children, 7 were initially without appropriate verbal behaviour. Five of the seven remained so after intensive treatment. In contrast, of the 6

TABLE 4

*Initial characteristics and later speech development
in children without communication when first assessed*
(includes cases and long-term controls)

Language level at follow-up	Initial Measures			
	Mean age (months)	Mecham age (months)	Mean IQ	Level of behavioural disturbance
Still mute (N = 5)	50.4	5.8	101.8	32.6
Some words/word Approximations (N = 5)	58.2	13.8	86.4	47.6
Some simple phrase or sentence speech (N = 2)	39.5	14.0	102.5	33.0

*   Based on ratings from parental reports. The lower the score the more "normal" the behaviour.

children who started with some speech, *all* made substantial gains*.

Particular interest concerns the differences in our group (and Lovaas') between the initially non-communicating children who remained mute and those who developed some speech. The numbers are too small and the measures too limited for much in the way of systematic comparisons but (see Table 4) the mean initial Mecham (1958) language age of the five who remained mute (5.8 months) was well below that for the five children who achieved some word combinations (13.8 months) or the two who gained phrase speech (14.0 months). Thus, the children who made no progress in their use of speech were extremely retarded in all their communication skills, they made very few spontaneous sounds, had little or no comprehension of spoken

*Incidentally it may be observed that this difference makes Lovaas' comparison of institution-treated and parent-treated children invalid so far as language changes are concerned. The groups were so different initially that this could explain the outcome variation.

language and showed no imitative skills. It is relevant to note that in this group (which excluded children with a non-verbal IQ below 60) that neither IQ nor level of behavioural disturbance predicted language development in initially mute children.

We may conclude that even quite prolonged and intensive behavioral treatment in the child's own home can do little to bring on language development when the initial linguistic and pre-linguistic skills are so profoundly retarded. We are reminded that the language impairment is part of a broader cognitive deficit of organic origin, and that treatment can improve performance but it cannot remove the basic handicap. Of course, that does not mean that our treatment programme was of no value for this most handicapped group. On the contrary, most children showed substantial and worthwhile social and behavioural gains. The point is simply that, in spite of these other gains, there was little alteration in the child's cognitive/linguistic deficit.

The very marked and sometimes dramatic, language gains of the children who started with just a little speech stand out in sharp contrast. This is the group for whom language training seems to have most to offer. I will return to the question of exactly what it achieves after discussing how language can be taught.

How can language be taught

Our home based treatment programme used a variety of techniques to aid children's language development but it relied heavily on the use of operant or reinforcement methods. It is clear from a host of studies that operant treatments have often been followed by improved speech production (see Yule and Berger, 1972; Guess *et al.*, 1974; Lovaas, 1977) but have they *specifically* influenced the development of *language* in the sense of a symbolic code that allows the generation of novel messages (Lewis, 1968)?

That is a more difficult question which involves several rather different issues. First, how can you be sure that it was indeed the specific treatment used (rather than biological maturation or experiences outside the therapeutic situation) which led to the gains in speech production? The only really satisfactory test is to teach the child some developmentally inappropriate or idiosyncratic aspect of language. In fact this has been done with reinforcement, modelling and imitation/ expansion techniques. Thus, Guess *et al.*, (1968) showed that reinforcement methods could be used to teach retarded children a *reversed* grammatical rule (namely add "s" for the singular and take off "s" for the plural); Malouf and Dodd (1972) demonstrated that imitations and expansions could be used to teach an artificial grammatical rule concerning word order; and Whitehurst *et al.*, (1974) used selective modelling to teach children passive constructions at an age when they are very rarely used. In all three cases the very *novelty* of the item learned demonstrated that the learning was indeed specifically due to the teaching given. Note, however, that the learning followed three apparently different techniques – reinforcement, expansion, and modelling.

The second question is whether they were learning language. This issue may be approached by determining the extent to which the rule learned is *generalised* and the extent to which it is used *spontaneously* in the child's creation of entirely new utterances. The evidence on both counts is rather inconclusive. All methods of training have been associated with the generalisation of the "rule" learned to words or constructions not specifically included in the teaching procedures. However, that observation does not take us very far as generalisations within a response *class* is a usual feature of operant learning (Skinner, 1953) and not anything specifically characteristic of language.

Guess and his colleagues (Guess *et al*, 1968; Guess, 1969; Guess and Baer, 1973) studied another kind of generalisation – that from comprehension to production and vice versa. They found very little generalisation between the two aspects of language. On the other hand, other investigators (Ruder and Smith, 1974) have found that training in one may help learning in the other.

A third kind of generalisation is that from the controlled training setting to the child's "natural environment" at home or at school (Guess *et al.*, 1974). Very little evidence is available on this point – indeed most studies have not only been concerned with just one setting but also have examined language production elicited in just one rather specific fashion. Nevertheless, our own study does show that generalisation across settings can and does occur if this is made an objective of training.

The last issue, of *spontaneous* and *novel* usage of what is learned, is, perhaps, specially important in connection with autism, as a lack of spontaneous usage is such a characteristic feature. Certainly, we have found, as have others (see e.g. Salzinger *et al.*, 1965; Lovaas, 1977), that *some* autistic children do go on to use language spontaneously, generating quite new word combinations which utilise the rules which have been taught. Nevertheless, it has also been found that most autistic children in training programmes, just like other autistic children, usually remain grossly impaired in their spontaneous language. Thus, Lovaas *et al.*, (1973) found that spontaneous verbal behaviour was consistently worse than elicited verbal behaviour. Moreover, when specific selective reinforcements were no longer given, language production deteriorated (Lovaas, 1977). It is all too evident that even years of training does *not* result in any kind of language "breakthrough" after which normal language development proceeds of its own accord as in other children. Nevertheless, it is also apparent the reinforcement techniques, like expansions, modelling and imitation, can aid the development of skills which show sufficient generalisation and spontaneous usage to claim that at least they contribute to true language.

How is language best taught?

We now need to turn to the even more difficult question of *which* of the various alternatives proposed is the *best* way to teach language (to ordinary *or* autistic children). It may be said straight away that the evidence on this point allows no firm conclusions. Three types of studies contribute to this discussion.

First, there are the cross-sectional naturalistic studies (e.g. Cross, 1977). These show quite strong correlations between the mother's and the child's spoken language. Thus, expansions, self-repetitions, stock phrases and references to the child's activities are all more frequently found when speaking to normal children with very limited linguistic skills. The findings have been used by Cross to argue that the mother's speech is, and needs to be, finely tuned to the child's current language capacity. Insofar as this is so, it implies that there cannot be *one* generally "best" way of teaching language but rather that the appropriate *mesh* between adult and child is the essential feature.

On the other hand, Tizard's studies of children in long-stay residential nurseries (Tizard *et al.*, 1972) suggest that language comprehension is facilitated by certain broad styles of adult-child interaction. Children were most likely to show good receptive language development when there was a high frequency of informative (rather than supervisory or controlling) staff talk; a high rate of answering the children's questions; and much active (rather than passive) play. The inference is that frequent active social and conversational interchange may facilitate language development.

Second, there are the longitudinal naturalistic studies. Nelson (1973) in an investigation of a socially homogeneous middle class sample found very little association between the form of the mother's speech (proportion of questions, length of utterance, etc.) and any aspect of children's language development. However, the number of adults the child was exposed to and the number of outings per week were both significantly and positively correlated with language development. Interestingly, the correlation with TV watching was negative. The evidence is weak but it suggests that active social interchanges (rather than any particular linguistic style) is the most important feature. Clarke-Stewart's (1973) findings also indicate that language development is positively correlated with maternal stimulation and responsiveness. Newport *et al.* (1977) found no consistent relationships between the child's language development and the complexity or length of the mother's utterances or the amount of repetition. The form of the mother's syntax was associated with some aspects of the child's grammar but not with other features of his language. Expansions seemed associated with language growth and so did an extensive use of feedback and reinforcement. Mothers tend to reinforce their children for the truth of what they say rather than its syntactic correctness (Brown and Hanlon, 1970) but, nevertheless, an ample provision of encouragement seems helpful.

Thirdly, there are the experimental studies. Irwin (1960) showed that reading to infants increased their babble, and Routh (1969) found that the form and amount of vocalisation could be influenced by contingent reinforcements. Interestingly, Dodd (1972) noted that babbling could be increased by combined social and vocal stimulation but not by either social or vocal stimulation on its own.

Brown, Cazden and Bellugi-Klima (1969) in an experimental study of young black children, compared the effects on language of expansion, modelling and non-verbal play. Modelling proved to be the most effective treatment. Nelson *et al.* (1973) compared the benefits of recast sentences (i.e. expansions and other sentence forms used to display new but related syntactic information) and new sentences (i.e. short grammatically, complete sentences which excluded the child's content words). Both groups showed more language gains than an untreated control group but the differences were fairly small and only the recast sentence-control differences reached statistical significance.

Murray (1972) found that a reciprocal exchange procedure was a more effective training technique than either modelling or expansions (both being rather narrowly defined). The advantages of the reciprocal exchange procedure were said to lie in its direct connection with what the child was saying.

We may tentatively conclude that children's language development is aided by active conversational interchange in a social context. Reinforcement, modelling, expansions and other conversational techniques have all proved helpful but so far there is no clear evidence to indicate whether any one technique has any marked advantage over the others.

As these comparative studies give only the most general guide as to how language is best taught, let us now return to the naturalistic situation and ask how parents normally talk to young children when they are first learning to speak. Perhaps that will provide some guidance.

Talking to Young Children

Numerous studies have shown that the way people talk to young children is strikingly different from adult conversations (Snow, 1977; Snow and Ferguson, 1977; Farwell, 1973; Vorster, 1975). These characteristics were first observed in mothers' talk to their infants and the style was sometimes termed "motherese". However, the style is not a function of being a parent as even children tend to adopt this distinctive style of talking to toddlers (Shatz and Gelman, 1973). Accordingly, the broader term "baby talk" seems preferable in spite of the fact that it leaves it ambiguous whether the baby is speaker or spoken to.

It does not necessarily follow that because people speak to young children in a particular style, that this style is optimal for teaching language. Nevertheless, it seems reasonable to suppose that a style which is rather consistent across different languages and cultures (Ferguson, 1977; Blount, 1972) might have some advantages. If so, it is desirable to provide some conceptual grouping of the main features of baby talk. Different writers have done this in slightly varying fashion but I suggest that three main headings bring out most of the crucial elements: (a) attention gaining and holding devices; (b) aids to conversational interchange; and (c) simplicity of processing. It will be appreciated that the use of these terms implies a purpose and readers will need to consider how far the inferences drawn are justified.

Attention gaining and holding devices

There is a strong tendency in "baby talk" to use a higher pitched voice as if to signal that now you are addressing the child (rather than anyone else in the room). The prosodic contours are exaggerated and there is a greater use of emphasis on key words (Garnica, 1977). Thus, in the sentence "push the red button" both "push" and "red" might be emphasised (*push* the *red* button) in order to bring the key words to the child's notice. Also, there may be a greater use of attentional words such as "see", "look" and "watch" (Shatz and Gelman, 1973). In addition, much use is made of *deictic* utterances in which a child's attention is drawn to some object in the environment by saying things like *"Here's* your giraffe" or *"That's* your nose" (Newport et al., 1977). There is an almost exclusive use of the present tense (Snow, 1977) and conversation tends to centre around the here and now environment. Mothers tend to speak about an object primarily when their young child is looking at it (Collis, 1975), a means of ensuring that the conversation focuses on items of interest to the child.

Moreover, there tends to be a high rate of repetition in what people say to young children: "Go get the duck – the duck – yes, get it – that's right – get the duck". It appears that the majority of such repetitions immediately follow the child's failure to respond or his misinterpretation of what was said (Cross, 1975). In this way the repetition serves both as an emphasis and as a communication check. All of these features may be considered as different ways of attracting and holding the child's attention – the first necessity if a conversational interchange is to follow.

Aids to conversational interchange

Secondly, "baby talk" includes a variety of elements which seem designed to encourage the child to respond, and hence to keep the conversation going. When talking to one another, adults use many "turn-keeping" devices, for example adding "well" or "but" at the end of a phrase to indicate that they want to go on holding the floor and are not yet ready for the other person to speak (Snow and Ferguson, 1977). These devices are rarely used in talking to children. Instead, there is a high use of interrogatives (what is that?) and imperatives (show me the car) which demand some kind of speech or social response (Snow, 1972: Newport *et al.*, 1977). Speech occurs within the context of social interchange and with young children there is a greater need to use turn passing devices to ensure that the child reciprocates and so keeps the conversation going.

Baby talk also includes a high rate of expansions (Newport *et al.*, 1977; Snow, 1977) in which the adult provides an adult version of the child's foreshortened or distorted attempt ("Book table" . . . "Yes, the book is on the table"). There has been much discussion in the literature on the role of expansions as a means of teaching grammar. However, they also seem to serve the purpose of providing general encouragement or reinforcement of the child's speaking, together with a means of checking the meaning of what the child has just said (Brown, 1977). In psychotherapy with adults reflective interpretations in which there is a sympathetic restatement of what the patient has just said have been shown to be reinforcing (Adams *et al.*, 1962: Noblin *et al.*, 1963). Perhaps, expansions are comparably reinforcing to young children. Maybe, it is not just the extra syntactic information in an expansion which is valuable but also the implicit reinforcing message to the child that the adult has heard, has understood, and has been interested or pleased with the child's communication.

Simplicity of processing

Thirdly, baby talk seems designed to provide simplicity of processing for an individual with a limited attention span and a limited
comprehension of language (Broen, 1972; Snow, 1972; Cross, 1977;
Newport *et al.*, 1977; Ferguson, 1977). Thus, people tend to speak
more slowly and to use shorter sentences when speaking to young
children. There is little use of subordinate clauses and most utterances
contain only one proposition. Articulation is usually clear and there are
fewer mumbled or unintelligible utterances than in adult conversation.
The vocabulary is kept simple and tends to be immediately related to
objects in the child's environment. Not only are sentences generally
much shorter but also there is a higher rate of incomplete sentences or
isolated phrases in baby talk. Thus, talk to children often includes
highly deleted phrases such as "wanna go out?" instead of *"do you*
want to go out?" or isolated comments such as "on the table"; both of
which are less common in adult conversation.

These last items are interesting and important in drawing attention
to the fact that "baby talk" is *not* syntactically simple. Deletions
increase the disparity between deep and surface structures (Newport *et*
al., 1977) and in its range of grammatical constructions baby talk is in
many ways more complicated than normal speech. However, it is well
designed for simplicity of processing in other respects. The short
sentences require only a brief memory span, the vocabulary makes few
semantic demands, the phonological clarity reduces ambiguity, and
the focus on the child's immediate environment aids understanding. It
is only in terms of grammar that "baby talk" seems possibly confusing.

However, other evidence suggests that this is not the crucial element
in effective communication with infants. Young children tend to pay
special attention to the beginnings of utterances and respond more
readily to abbreviated instructions such as "throw ball" than to fully
grammatical adult commands (Shipley *et al.*, 1969). Interestingly,
Wetstone and Friedlander (1973) found that very young children with
non-fluent language responded as well to scrambled as to normal
sentences. Apparently, to a two-year-old it is as effective to say "box
the up open" as to say "open up the box"! At this early stage of
language acquisition (but not later) the meaning comes much more

from the word content and from the social context than from the grammar.

Teaching Language to Autistic Children

These considerations have taken us rather a long way from the problem of teaching language to autistic children. It is necessary now to try to draw the threads together to see what conclusions follow from these rather diverse studies. It appears that an effective treatment method is likely to involve eight main components.

First, if it is necessary when talking to young *normal* children to use devices to gain and hold their attention, this is likely to be much more the case with autistic children. A lack of response to the human voice and a lack of socially determined eye to eye gaze are two of the most striking features of the autistic syndrome in young children (Rutter, 1978b). Moreover, stereotyped repetitive movements and other deviant behaviours frequently interfere with normal social interaction. Accordingly, the first task in treatment is to gain the child's attention. Selective social reinforcement may be used to encourage children to attend. Reinforcement techniques or graded change may also be employed to reduce rituals or stereotypies which interfere with social involvement. Also, it is important to ensure success in whatever tasks the child is given. Failure not only leads to impaired social responsiveness (Churchill, 1971; Koegel and Covert, 1972) but also it is likely to increase stereotyped responses which interfere with learning and cognitive performance (Clark and Rutter, 1979).

Second, language is a code for communication which is most readily learned by conversational interchange in a social context. Almost all studies indicate that steps to increase this linguistic social interaction are likely to facilitate the child's language development. This is a particular problem with autistic children who not only fail to engage in social interaction but also fail to use what language they possess for social purposes. If they are to learn language in optimal fashion they need to be helped to engage in and to enjoy social interaction. There is continuing controversy in the literature about how this is best achieved (Richer, 1978; Howlin, 1978; Rutter and Sussenwein, 1971), but we have found that a socially intrusive approach combined with effective social reinforcement (based on an analysis of what is *actually* rewarding to the child) works well (Hemsley *et al.*, 1978; Rutter *et al.*, 1977). As with young children, it is also necessary to use a style of communication which encourages the child to respond. The form of speech is relevant (both questions and requests are more likely than declarative statements to bring a response), but there is also a need to give strong encouragement and approval when the child does respond.

Third, the level of linguistic input must be appropriate to the level of the child's understanding of language. As with normal children, it is probably not the syntactic complexity which is most important but rather the overall meaning of the utterance which is crucial. If the language environment provided for the child is to be beneficial it must impinge and be meaningful. Thus, it has been found that children with limited language comprehension make better progress when spoken to in short, rather than long, sentences (Browning, 1974).

Fourth, no one linguistic technique provides all the answers in the actual procedure of teaching language. Reinforcement techniques have an important role to play but so also do modelling, imitation, expansion and other feedback methods, as well as just ordinary conversational interchange about here and now activities of interest to the child.

Fifth, as Bricker and Bricker (1974) emphasise, there is evidence of the importance of prelinguistic forms of behaviour for subsequent language development. They may constitute the necessary basis for the development of spoken language. It is important not only to focus on the genesis of speech but also to pay attention to imitation, make-believe play and language comprehension. Receptive language training is important in its own right (Guess *et al.*, 1968, 1973, 1974 studies – see above – indicate that comprehension does not necessarily develop with production), but also it may aid expressive language skills (Pothier *et al.*, 1974).

Sixth, it is communication which is important and if speech is proving too difficult there should be recourse to other language modalities. Thus, it may be worthwhile developing gesture both to facilitate the child's understanding (Webster *et al.*, 1973) and to provide one particular means of communication (Fenn and Rowe, 1975).

Seventh, it is necessary to plan treatment in such a way as to encourage generalisation across settings (Wulbert *et al.*, 1974) and to encourage spontaneous social usage. Working closely with parents (Lansing and Schopler, 1978), and seeing the family in their own home (Hemsley *et al.*, 1978) are likely to help.

Eighth, there is a need to give the child skills which will enable him to *continue* learning language *outside* the therapeutic sessions. Teaching him to attend to other people and to engage in social interaction are both crucial in this connection but probably so also is the development of generalised imitation (Baer and Sherman, 1964).

Conclusions: How does it Work and what does it Achieve?

That brings me back to the questions with which I started. How does language training with autistic children work and what does it achieve? With regard to the first question, I do not believe that there is any one mechanism which accounts for the whole process. Reinforcement techniques undoubtedly constitute a most powerful and useful tool which is probably an indispensable element in any effective programme. Most of all, reinforcement methods are needed in bringing about the reciprocal social interaction (free of distracting deviant behaviours) which forms the necessary context within which to learn language. They are also useful in the process of teaching the child individual language skills but here they probably constitute but one of several effective strategies. There is no evidence as yet to indicate how far they are better or worse than other techniques which have their origin in psycholinguistics rather than learning theory. However, it would be quite wrong to see these approaches as in opposition to one another. Already, there has been a considerable rapprochement between the two, and most therapists utilise methods which draw from both theoretical backgrounds (Staats, 1974). It makes good sense to base language intervention strategies on what is known of normal language development (Miller and Yoder, 1974), but it remains to be determined whether language is best taught to autistic children in the same way that normal children learn it. After all, the distinctive feature of autistic language is not so much its delay as its deviance.

What is needed is a comparison of different approaches to language training as applied to the same type of language problems, along with a study of their longitudinal effects (Horton, 1974; Guess *et al.*, 1974). There is also a need to examine the possibility that the existing behaviours of the language deficient child might serve as predictor variables for the selection of the best training techniques for that child (Guess *et al.*, 1974).

Reinforcement techniques have proved very useful in the treatment of children with severe language delay and deviance, and yet there are considerable difficulties in explaining the whole of language development in terms of differential reinforcement (see Cromer, Chapter 1). It might seem useful to consider just how far the various aspects of language are actually learned by means of reinforcement, but this would not be very productive. The reason is that reinforcement theory is, by its nature, a circular or tautological theory. Reinforcement cannot be defined in terms which are independent of its effects and, as Bricker and Bricker (1974) point out, this means that it is almost impossible to reject (and therefore to test) the theory. However, the strength of operant conditioning does not lie in its force as an overall theory but rather in its power to give rise to practical techniques to influence behaviour. As such it can be and should be utilised to increase the efficacy of any training procedure.

Finally, what does the language training of autistic children achieve? Clearly, the results are more modest than some enthusiasts would have us believe (Lovaas, 1977). On the other hand, something useful is achieved, particularly in those autistic children who have some minimal language skills to begin with. The short-term benefits of treatment are obvious and in the longer term something useful is gained in increasing the social and communicative use of language (which, after all, is what language is all about). It seems possible that treatment may also accelerate at least the early stages of language development. Whether it modifies the final level of language competence reached is more dubious – but it may do so in a few cases. If it does so, the question is whether this is because reinforcement techniques have built up a bigger repertoire of language skills item by item, or rather whether the gains come from giving the autistic child some of the skills needed for him to learn language better himself. It is possible that this latter result could stem from improved social interaction and generalised imitation skills. It may be, too, that giving the child a few basic items of language through specific teaching helps to make him a more rewarding child for his parents and other adults to interact with. Talking to a socially unresponsive mute child is a singularly unrewarding exercise and the transformation into a child who intermittently reinforces the parent with the odd word could make quite a difference.

However, these last suggestions are speculative and we have to admit that we do not yet know just how much can be achieved by providing autistic children with language training. Something worthwhile, certainly, but equally certainly we cannot usually overcome basic handicaps. Nevertheless, it would be wrong to suppose that we have yet done all that can be done. As I have tried to indicate, there are still many avenues to explore in developing effective strategies to aid language development.

Acknowledgements

The home based project was a collaborative study with M. Berger, W. Yule, L. Hersov, R. Hemsley, P. Howlin and D. Holbrook. supported by a grant from the DHSS.

References

Adams, H.E., Butler, J. and Noblin, C.D. (1962) Effects of psychoanalytically derived interpretations: a verbal conditioning paradigm, *Psychol. Rep.*, **10**, 691–94.
Baer, D.M. and Sherman, J.A. (1964) Reinforcement control of generalized imitation in young children, *J. Exp. Child. Psychol.*, **1**, 37–49.
Bartak, L. and Rutter, M. (1976) Differences between mentally retarded and normally intelligent autistic children, *J. Autism Child. Schiz.*, **6**, 109–20.
Bartak, L., Rutter, M. and Cox, A. (1975) A comparative study of infantile autism and specific developmental receptive language disorder, I. The Children, *Brit. J. Psychiat.*, **126**, 127–45.
Bartak, L., Rutter, M. and Cox, A. (1977) A comparative study of infantile autism and specific developmental receptive language disorders, III. Discriminant function analysis, *J. Autism Child. Schiz.*, **7**, 383–96.
Blount, B.G. (1972) Parental speech and language acquisition: some Luo and Samson

examples, *Anthropological Linguistics,* 14, 119–30.

Bricker, W.A. and Bricker, D.D. (1974) An early language training strategy, *In: Language Perspectives — Acquisition, Retardation, and Intervention,* R. L. Schiefelbusch and L.L. Lloyds (eds.), Macmillan, London, pp 615–46.

Broen, P. (1972) The verbal environment of the language-learning child, *Monogr. American Speech. Hear. Assoc.* No. 17.

Brown, R. (1977) Introduction, *In: Talking to Children: Language Input and Acquisition,* C.E. Snow and C.A. Ferguson (eds.), Cambridge University Press, Cambridge, pp 1–27.

Brown, R., Cazden, C. and Bellugi-Klima, H. (1969) The child's grammar from I to III, *In: Minnesota Symposia on Child Psychology, Vol. 2.* J. P. Hill (ed.) University of Minnesota Press, Minneapolis, pp 28–73.

Brown, R. and Hanlon, C. (1970) Derivational complexity and order of acquisition in child speech. *In: Cognition and the Development of Language,* J. R. Hayes (ed.), Wiley, New York.

Browning, E.R. (1974) The effectiveness of long and short verbal commands in inducing correct responses in three schizophrenic children, *J. Autism Child. Schiz.,* 4, 293–300.

Cantwell, D., Baker, L. and Rutter, M. (1978) A comparative study of infantile autism and specific developmental receptive language disorder, IV. Syntactical and functional analysis of language, *J. Child Psychol. Psychiat.* 19, 351–62.

Cantwell, D., Howlin, P. and Rutter, M. (1977) The analysis of language level and language function: a methodological study, *Brit. J. Disord. Commun.,* 12, 119–35.

Churchill, D.W. (1971) Effects of success and failure in psychotic children, *Arch. gen. psychiat.,* 25, 208–14.

Clark, P. and Rutter, M. (1977) Compliance and resistance in autistic children, *J. Autism Child. Schiz.,* 7, 33–48.

Clark, P. and Rutter, M. (1979) Task difficulty and task performance in autistic children *J. Child Psychol. Psychiat.* 20, 271–85.

Clarke-Stewart, K.A. (1973) Interactions between mothers and their young children: characteristics and consequences, *Monogr. Soc. Res. Child Develop.,* 38, Serial No. 153.

Collis, G. (1975) The integration of gaze and vocal behaviour in the mother-infant dyad, Cited by Newport *et al.,* 1977.

Cross, T.G. (1975) Some relationships between motherese and linguistic level in accelerated children, *Papers and Reports on Child Language Development No. 10,* Stanford University, Stanford, California.

Cross, T.G. (1977) Mothers' speech adjustments: the contribution of selected child listener variables, *In: Talking to Children: Language Input and Acquisition,* by C.E. Snow and C.A. Ferguson (eds.), Cambridge University Press, Cambridge, pp 151–88.

Dodd, B.J. (1972) Effects of social and vocal stimulation on infant babbling, *Develop. Psychol.,* 7, 80–83.

Farwell, C. (1973) The language spoken to children, *Papers and Reports on Child Language Development,* No. 5, pp 31–62, Stanford University, Stanford, California.

Fenn, G. and Rowe, J.A. (1975) An experiment in manual communication, *Brit. J. Dis. Commun.,* 10, 3–16.

Ferguson, C.A. (1977) Baby talk as a simplified register, *In: Talking to Children: Language Input and Acquisition*, C.E. Snow and C.A. Ferguson (eds.), Cambridge University Press, Cambridge, pp 219–36.

Folstein, S. and Rutter, M. (1977) Infantile autism: A genetic study of 21 twin pairs, *J. Child Psychol. Psychiat.*, **18**, 297–321.

Garnica, O.K. (1977) Some prosodic and paralinguistic features of speech to young children, *In: Talking to Children: Language Input and Acquisition*, C.E. Snow and C.A. Ferguson (eds.), Cambridge University Press, Cambridge, pp 63–88.

Guess, D. (1969) A functional analysis of receptive and productive speech: acquisition of the plural morpheme, *J. appl. Behav. Analysis*, **2**, 55–64.

Guess, D. and Baer, D.M. (1973) An analysis of individual differences in generalization between receptive and productive language in retarded children, *J. app. Behav. Analysis*, **6**, 311–29.

Guess, D., Sailor, W. and Baer, D.M. (1974) To teach language to retarded children. *In: Language Perspectives — Acquisition, Retardation, and Intervention*, R.L. Schiefelbusch & L.L. Lloyds (eds.), Macmillan, London, pp 529–64.

Guess, D., Sailor, W., Rutherford, G. and Baer, D.M. (1968) An experimental analysis of linguistic development: the productive use of the plural morpheme, *J. app. Behav. Analysis*, **1**, 225–35.

Hemsley, R., Howlin, P., Berger, M., Hersov, L., Holbrook, D., Rutter, M. and Yule, W. (1978) Treating autistic children in a family context, *In: Autism: A Reappraisal of Concepts and Treatment*, M. Rutter and E. Schopler (eds.), Plenum, New York.

Hermelin, B. and O'Connor, N. (1970) *Psychological Experiments with Autistic Children*, Pergamon, Oxford.

Horton, K.B. (1974) Infant intervention and language learning, *In: Language Perspectives — Acquisition, Retardation, and Intervention*, R.L. Schiefelbusch and L. L. Lloyds (eds.), Macmillan, London, pp 469–92.

Howlin, P. (1978) The assessment of social behaviour, *In: Autism: A Reappraisal of Concepts and Treatment*, M. Rutter and E. Schopler (eds.), Plenum, New York.

Irwin, O.C. (1960) Infant speech: effect of systematic reading of stories. *J. Speech Hear. Res.*, **3**, 187–90.

Kazdin, A.E. (1973) Methodological and assessment considerations in evaluating reinforcement programs in applied settings, *J. appl. Behav. Analysis*, **6**, 517–31.

Koegel, R.L. and Covert, A. (1972) The relationship of self-stimulation to learning in autistic children. *J. Appl. Behav. Anal.*, **5**, 381–7.

Lansing, M. and Schopler, E. (1978) Individualized education: A public school model, *In Autism: A Reappraisal of Concepts and Treatment*, M. Rutter and E. Schopler (eds.), Plenum, New York.

Lewis, M. (1968) Language and mental development, *In: Development in Human Learning II*, E. A. Lunzer and J. F. Morris (eds.), Staples Press, London. p. 68.

Lovaas, O.I. (1977) *The Autistic Child: Language Development Through Behaviour Modification*, Wiley, New York.

Lovaas, O.I., Koegel, R., Simmons, J.Q. and Long, J.S. (1973) Some generalization and follow-up measures on autistic children in behaviour therapy. *J. appl. Behav. Analysis*, **6**, 131–66.

Malouf, R.E. and Dodd, D.H. (1972) Role of exposure, imitation, and expansion in the acquisition of an artificial grammatical rule, *Develop. Psychol.*, **7**, 195–203.

Mecham, M.J. (1958) *Verbal Language Developmental Scale,* Educational Test Bureau, Minneapolis.

Miller, J.F. and Yoder, D.E. (1974) An ontogenetic language teaching strategy for retarded children, *In: Language Perspectives — Acquisition, Retardation, and Intervention,* R.L. Schiefelbusch and L.L. Lloyds (eds.), Macmillan, London, pp 505–28.

Murray, S. (1972) Investigation of three teaching methods for language training. Unpublished doctoral dissertation, University of Kansas, cited by Ruder, K.F. and Smith, M.D. (1974).

Nelson, K. (1973) Structure and strategy in learning to talk, *Monogr. Soc. Res. Child Develop.,* **38**, Serial No. 149.

Nelson, K.E., Carskaddon, G. and Bonvillian, J.D. (1973) Syntax acquisition: impact of experimental variation in adult verbal interaction with the child, *Child Develop.,* **44**, 497–504.

Newport, E.L., Gleitman, H. and Gleitman, L.R. (1977) Mother, I'd rather do it myself: some effects and non-effects of maternal speech style, *In: Talking to Children: Language Input and Acquisition,* C.E. Snow & C.A. Ferguson (eds.), Cambridge University Press, Cambridge, pp 109–49.

Noblin, C.D., Timmons, E.O. and Reynard, M.C. (1963) Psychoanalytic interpretations as verbal reinforcers: importance of interpretation content, *J. Clin. Psychol.,* **19**, 479–81.

Pothier, P., Morrison, D. and Gorman, F. (1974) Effects of receptive language training on receptive and expressive language development, *J. Abnorm. Child. Psychol.,* **2**, 153–64.

Reynell, J. (1969) Test Manual, Reynell Developmental Language Scales, Experimental Edition N.F.E.R. Slough.

Richer, J. (1978) The partial non-communication of culture to autistic children — an application of human ethology, *In: Autism: A Reappraisal of Concepts and Treatment,* M. Rutter & E. Schopler (eds.), Plenum, New York.

Routh, D.K. (1969) Conditioning of vocal response differentiation in infants, *Develop. Psychol.,* **1**, 219–226.

Ruder, K.F. and Smith, M.D. (1974) Issues in language training, *In: Language Perspectives — Acquisition, Retardation, and Intervention,* R.L. Schiefelsbusch & L.L. Lloyds (eds.), Macmillan, London, pp 565–606.

Rutter, M. (1978) Diagnosis and definition, *In: Autism: A Reappraisal of Concepts and Treatment,* M. Rutter & E. Schoper (eds.), Plenum, New York.

Rutter, M. (1979) Autism: Psychopathological mechanisms and therapeutic approaches, *In: Cognitive Growth and Development — Essays in memory of Herbert G. Birch,* M. Bortner (ed.), Brunner/Mazel, New York.

Rutter, M. and Sussenwein, F. (1971) A developmental and behavioural approach to the treatment of pre-school autistic children, *J. Autism Child. Schiz.,* **1**, 376–97.

Rutter, M., Yule, W., Berger, M. and Hersov, L. (1977) An Evaluation of a Behavioural Approach to the Treatment of Autistic Children. Final Report to the Department of Health & Social Security, London.

Salzinger, K., Feldman, R., Cowan, J. and Salzinger, S. (1965) Operant conditioning of verbal behaviour of two young speech deficient boys, *In: Case Studies in Behaviour Modification,* L.P. Ullman & L. Frasner (eds.), Holt, Rinehart & Winston, New York.

Shatz, M. and Gelman, R. (1973) The development of communication skills: modifications in the speech of young children as a function of listener, *Monogr. Soc. Res. Child Develop.*, **38**, Serial No. 152.

Shipley, E.F., Smith, C.S. and Gleitman, L.R. (1969) A study in the acquisition of language: free response to commands, *Language*, **45**, 322–34.

Skinner, B.F. (1953) *Science and Human Behaviour*, Macmillan, New York.

Snow, C.E. (1972) Mothers' speech to children learning language, *Child Develop.*, **43**, 549–65.

Snow, C.E. (1977) The Development of conversation between mothers and babies, *J. Child. Lang.*, **4**, 1–22.

Snow, C.E. and Ferguson, C.A. (eds.) (1977) *Talking to Children: Language Input and Acquisition*, Cambridge University Press, Cambridge.

Staats, A.W. (1974) Behaviorism and cognitive theory in the study of language: a neopsycholinguistics, *In: Language Perspectives — Acquisition, Retardation, and Intervention*, Macmillan, London, pp 615–46.

Tizard, B., Cooperman, O., Joseph, A. and Tizard, J. (1972) Environmental effects on language development: A study of young children in long-stay residential nurseries, *Child Develop.*, **43**, 337–58.

Vorster, J. (1975) Mommy linguist: the case for motherese, *Lingua*, **37**, 281–312.

Webster, C.D., McPherson, H., Sloman, L., Evans, M.A. and Kuchar, E. (1973) Communicating with an autistic boy by gestures, *J. Autism Child. Schiz.*, **3**, 337–46.

Wetstone, H.S. and Friedlander, B.Z. (1973) The effect of word order on young children's responses to simple questions and commands, *Child Develop.*, **44**, 734–40.

Whitehurst, G.J., Ironsmith, M. and Goldfein, M. (1974) Selective imitation of the passive construction through modeling, *J. exp. Child Psychol.*, **17**, 288–302.

Wulbert, M., Barach, R., Perry, M., Straughan, J., Sulbacher, S., Turner, K. and Wiltz, N. (1974) The generalization of newly acquired behaviours by parents and child across three different settings: A study of an autistic child, *J. Abnorm. Child Psychol.*, **2**, 87–98.

Yule, W. and Berger, M. (1972) Behaviour modification principles and speech delay, *In: The Child with Delayed Speech*, M. Rutter & J.A.M. Martin (eds.), Clinics in Developmental Medicine No. 43, SIMP/Heinemann, London, pp 204–19.

Author Index

173

Subject Index